GW00888799

nobu now

nobu matsuhisa

photography by eiichi takahashi

quadrille

sashimi

hot appetizers

soup

cold appetizers

salad

Contents

Cold Appetizers 14

Oyster Salmon Roll *16*, 18

White Asparagus and Sea Bass Sashimi with
   Mint Dressing *17*, 18

Monkfish Pâté with Caviar and Vinegar
   Mustard Sauce 19

Lotus Root Chips with Tuna and White Fish
   20, 24

Seared Toro Tartar *22*, 24

Squid Somen and Hearts of Palm 25, *26*

Sweet Shrimp Tartar with Caviar 25, *27*

Pen Shell Clam with Caviar *28*, 30

Nobu's Octopus Carpaccio *29*, 30

Mussels and Clams with Nobu's Salsas 32

Fruit Tomato and Vegetable Ceviche *34*, 36

Salmon Kelp Roll *35*, 36

Oyster and Sea Urchin Shooter 37

Hot Appetizers 38

Tuna Sashimi Tempura Roll with
   Yuzu Miso Sauce 41

Baby Turban Shells with Escargot
   Butter Sauce *42*, 44

Parmesan Baked Small Scallops *43*, 44

Quick Simmered Baby Octopus 45, *46*

Baby Scallop Skewers with Vegetable Salsa
   45, *47*

Minced Baby White Shrimp Skewers 49

Hot Ceviche *50*, *51*, 52

Shrimp and Asparagus with Egg Sauce 53, *54*

Deep-fried Toro Tataki with Spicy Garlic Sauce
   53, *55*

Kuruma Shrimp Roll 56

Salad 58

Fruit Tomato with Cilantro Sauce *61*, 62

Spicy Tuna Salad 63, *64*

Baby Spinach Salad with Sea Bass 63, *65*

Octopus and Molokheiya Salad *66*, 68

Tuna Tataki Sashimi Salad with Matsuhisa
   Dressing *67*, 68

Watercress and White Asparagus Salad with
   Watercress Dressing 70

Salmon Skin Salad 73

Page numbers in italics indicate recipe illustrated
on pages not alongside its text.

Sashimi 74

Snapper Sashimi with Dried Miso 76

Oyster Tiradito *78*, 82

Kobe Beef New-Style Sashimi *80*, 82

Bonito Tataki with Home-cured Anchovies *81*, 83

Scallop Tiradito 85

Toro with Jalapeño and Sumiso Sauce 86

Soup 88

Abalone Somen and Junsai Cold Soup 91

Matsutake Kettle Soup *92*, 94

Spicy Seafood Soup *93*, 95

Baby Ayu Soup 97

Fry 98

Deepfried Soft Shell Crab with Cactus Salsa *100*, 102

Soft Shell Crab Spring Roll *101*, 102

King Crab Claw Tempura with Butter Ponzu Sauce 103, *104*

King Crab Tempura with Sweet and Sour Ponzu Sauce 103, *105*

Rock Shrimp Tempura with Creamy Spicy Sauce *106*, 108

Japanese Shad Namban Style *107*, 109

Baby Ice Fish Fritter 109, *110–11*

Oyster Filo 112

Abalone Tempura *114–5*, 116

Sea Urchin and Corn Khakiage 116

Sea Eel "Fish & Chips" *118*, 120

Fish Skin Chips *119*, 121

Steam 122

Sea Urchin Pudding 124

Shark's Fin and Sea Urchin Pudding 126

Avocado Egg Pudding 128

Ray Fin with Spicy Black Bean Sauce *130*, 132

Moromi-Miso Mackerel *131*, 132

Tofu with Matsuhisa Dressing 133

Steamed Kinki Yuba Roll 135

Sauté 136

Fois Gras with Miso 138

Hamo and Fois Gras with Japanese Truffle Sauce
140, 143

Tuna Cheek with Shark's Fin Black Bean Sauce
141, 143

Garlic Sautéed Kuruma Shrimp 144, 146

Sautéed Razor Clam 145, 147

Chinese Cabbage Steak 149

Deep-fried Halibut Cheek with Black Peeper
Chili Garlic Sauce 150, 152

Sautéed Horse Mackerel with Spicy Lemon
Dressing 151, 152

King Crab with Creamy Spicy Sauce 153, 154

Mushroom Toban Yaki 153, 155

King Crab White Soufflé with Truffle 156, 159

Scallop and Brussels Sprouts with Jalapeño Salsa
157, 159

Miru Clam and Yuba Sauté 160

Grill 162

Kobe Beef Steak with Baked Eringi Mushrooms
164

Kobe Beef with Anti-cucho Sauce 167

Ise Lobster with Spicy Lemon Garlic Sauce 168,
170

Black Cod with Miso 169, 171

Lamb Chop with Miso Anti-cucho Sauce 173

Bamboo Roasted Ayu with Green and Red Tade
Sauces 174, 176

Grilled Salmon with Baby Spinach Chips 175,
176

Grilled Koyari Squid 177, 178

Black Pepper Crusted Black Cod 177, 179

Broiled Toro Back 180, 182

Grilled Chicken with Wasabi Pepper Sauce 181,
183

Makomo-Dake with Creamy Spicy Sauce 183,
184

Sushi 186

Nobu Style Assorted Sushi and Rolls 189

Vinegared Sushi Rice 190

Seafood Bara Sushi 191, 192–3

Soft Shell Crab Roll 194, 196

Salmon Skin Roll 195, 196

Funa Sushi Nobu Style 198

Soba 200

White Fish Somen with Pomodoro Sauce 203
Jalapeño Soba 204
Tade Soba *208*, 209
Coriander Soba *208*, 209
Lobster Inaniwa Pasta Salad 210

Rice 212

Black and Red Rice Risotto 214
Kabayaki Sardine Don *216*, 218
Aroz con Pollo *217*, 218

Desserts 220

Bamboo Jello *222*, 224–5
Banana Egg Roll 226–9
Passion Fruit Pasta 230–232
Layered Hazelnut Cake *233*, 234–5
Yuzu Soup with Apricot Ice Cream 237
Fruit Saké 238

Sauces 240

Red Anti-cucho (Aji Panca) Sauce 242
Ornage Anti-cucho (Aji Amarillo) Sauce 242
Creamy Spicy Sauce 242
Spicy Garlic Sauce 243
Spicy Lemon Garlic Sauce 243
Ceviche Sauce 243
Teriyaki Balsamic Sauce 243
Butter Ponzu Sauce 244
Yuzu Soy Sauce 244
Wasabi Soy Sauce 244
Tosazu Vinegar 244
Wasabi Pepper Sauce 244
Mustard Miso 245
Nobu-Style Saikyo Sweet Miso 245
Mustard Vinegar Miso Sauce 245

Dressings 246

Spicy Lemon Dressing 246
Watercress Dressing 246
Jalapeño Dressing 246
Yuzu Dressing 246
Matsuhisa Dressing 247

Salsas 247

Jalapeño Salsa 247
Maui Onion Salsa 247
Matsuhisa Salsa 247

Glossary 250

Index 253

cold appetizers

オイスターサーモンロール
Oyster Salmon Roll

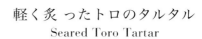

軽く炙ったトロのタルタル
Seared Toro Tartar

23

白身とマグロのレンコンチップ
Lotus Root Chips with Tuna and White Fish

Sashimi of white fish and red meat tuna are here combined with lotus root chips to create a truly novel food experience.

serves 1

1¾ ounces (50g) lotus root
rice vinegar
vegetable oil, for deep-frying
3 skinless boneless slices sea bass, each about ¼ ounce (8g)
3 skinless boneless slices red meat tuna, each about ¼ ounce
  (8g)
1½ large shiso leaves
a little Mustard Miso (see page 245)
Yuzu Miso Sauce (see page 41)

1   Peel off the lotus root skin, cut the root into 6 thin round slices and leave to soak in water with a few drops of vinegar for an hour or two. Drain and pat dry with paper towels.

2   Heat the oil for deep-frying to a temperature of 320°F (160°C). Fry the lotus root slices until they float to the surface and turn golden brown and crisp, then scoop out of the oil and place on paper towel to drain.

3   Cut both the sea bass and the tuna into slices about ⅛ inch (5mm) thick, then roll them, and arrange in separate bundles.

4   Make the Mustard Miso and the Yuzu Miso Sauce as described on pages 245 and 41 respectively.

5   Lay out the fried lotus chips. Cut the shiso leaves into quarters and place one on each chip, then arrange either a sea bass or tuna roll on top. Pour a little Mustard Miso on the tuna rolls and a little Yuzu Miso Sauce on the sea bass rolls.

NOBU'S NOTE
* Any firm white fish, such as sea bream or flounder, can be substituted for the sea bass.

軽く炙ったトロのタルタル
Seared Toro Tartar

Plump toro or tuna belly is given a more intense aroma and flavor when seared lightly after mixing it with some aromatic ingredients. The toro is served with a little caviar.

serves 1

2 ounces (60g) toro fillet (ask for the skin as well)
½ teaspoon finely chopped onions
¼ teaspoon finely chopped garlic
1 teaspoon caviar
chopped scallion (spring onion) greens
2 tablespoons Wasabi Soy Sauce (see page 244)
bamboo shoot leaves for garnish

1   Remove any sinews from the toro fillet using tweezers; if the meat sticks, scrape it off the sinews with a spoon (you can get your fishmonger to do this for you). Thinly slice the toro across and then lengthways, and then chop finely.

2   Using a spoon, mix the finely chopped onions and garlic with the toro, then put the mixture into a metal circular mold 2 inches (5cm) in diameter and 1 inch (2.5cm) in height. Place on a metal tray.

3   Preheat a dry non-stick pan until very hot. Lift the mold of the toro mixture and lightly sear the toro on all sides in the hot pan.

4   Chill the seared toro in the freezer for 10 to 15 minutes, so that the meat pieces do not fall apart.

5   Remove the toro from the freezer and take a thin slice off the top surface for appearance.

6   Place the toro in a small glass bowl and top it with caviar and a heap of scallion (spring onion). Pour the Wasabi Soy Sauce around it and half-bury the bowl in ice. Garnish with the rolled tuna skin and leaves from a bamboo shoot.

NOBU'S NOTES
* Do not chop the toro too finely.
* It is easier to slice the top surface off the toro after the mixture has been chilled in the freezer.

イカ素麺とハーツオブパーム
Squid Somen and Hearts of Palm

Popular squid somen paired with fresh hearts of young palm
have a really special flavor when eaten with soba dipping sauce.

serves 2
1 yariika squid
3½ ounces (100g) fresh hearts of young palm (palmetto)
sansho sprigs for garnish
soba dipping sauce (see Jalapeño Soba, page 205)

1   Remove the gut and the tentacles from the squid. Peel off
the top membrane and slice open the squid. Cut off about a
quarter of the pointed part to make a rectangle. Then, using the
tip of the knife, cut this lengthways to produce strips about ¹⁄₁₆
inch (1mm) wide.
2   Briefly dip the squid strips into boiling water and then
immediately plunge them into iced water to chill. Drain in a
colander.
3   Peel the hard skin from the palm hearts and shave the
hearts into thin slices. Plunge the slices into iced water and drain
in a colander.
4   Spread the hearts of palm on a plate and place the squid
somen on top. Place the sansho sprigs on one palm and pat
sharply once with the other palm to bring out their fragrance.
Place the sansho sprigs on top of the somen. Serve with the
soba dipping sauce.

NOBU'S NOTE
*   Hearts of young palm (palmetto) are the young shoots of
    palm trees, which are cooked, soaked in water mixed with
    salt and citric acid, and then bottled or canned. Fresh ones
    are crispy and taste somewhat different.

甘海老のタルタル　キャビア添え
Sweet Shrimp Tartar with Caviar

The tartar treatment brings out the delicate flavor of sweet
shrimp (prawns). This is one of those recipes suitable only for the
very freshest of sashimi fish.

serves 1
8 raw sweet shrimp (prawns) in the shell
½ teaspoon finely chopped onions
¼ teaspoon finely chopped garlic
⅛ ounce (5g) caviar
2 tablespoons Wasabi Soy Sauce (see page 244)

1   Shell the shrimp (prawns) and remove the heads and tails.
Finely chop the meat with a knife, taking care to leave some
chunks for texture. Add the onion and garlic and mix well. Pack
the mixture into a circular mold.
2   Unmold the mixture on to a small deep plate or a bowl.
Top with caviar and pour the Wasabi Soy Sauce around it.

NOBU'S NOTES
*   Chives cut into lengths of 2–2 ⅜ inches (5–6 cm) can
    be placed beside the shrimp tartar. Alternatively, a shrimp
    (prawn) tail and something green would make the
    presentation beautifully colorful.
*   The tartar will have a better texture if it is not chopped
    too finely.

イカ素麺とハーツオブパーム
Squid Somen and Hearts of Palm

甘海老のタルタル　キャビア添え
Sweet Shrimp Tartar with Caviar

平貝とキャビア
Pen Shell Clam with Caviar

マッスルと大アサリのサルサ2種
Mussels and Clams with Nobu's Salsas

The mussels and clams are cooked quickly and then enjoyed with two kinds of freshly made original salsas.

serves 2

2 large clams

4 large mussels

11 fluid ounces (330ml) Matsuhisa Salsa (see page 247)

15 fluid ounces (425ml) Maui Onion Salsa (see page 247)

finely chopped chives

1   Extract the clams from their shells and plunge them briefly into boiling well-salted water. Then plunge them into iced water to chill them quickly.

2   Plunge the mussels in their shells into boiling well-salted water. Take out the ones whose shells start to open and quickly chill them in iced water. Open the shells.

3   Make the Matsuhisa Salsa and Maui Onion Salsa as described on page 247.

4   Cut the clams in half and discard the innards. Place the clam meat back in their shells, spoon the Maui Onion Salsa on top, and arrange the chopped chives in the center. Spoon the Matsuhisa Salsa over the mussels in their shells.

5   Arrange the shells on crushed ice in a dish. Green leaves or something similar can be used for decoration.

NOBU'S NOTES

* Discard any open shells that don't close when tapped.
* Be careful not to cook shellfish for too long. Remove the mussels from the heat as soon as the shells open.
* Use only freshly made salsas.

フルーツトマトと季節の野菜のセビーチェ
Fruit Tomato and Vegetable Ceviche

サーモンケルプ　ロール
Salmon Kelp Roll

フルーツトマトと季節の野菜のセビーチェ
Fruit Tomato and Vegetable Ceviche

Ceviche Sauce is the decisive element of this dish. Abundant use of seasonal vegetables ensures good strong flavors and textures on the plate.

serves 2
¼ red onion
3 okra
2 fruit tomatoes
1 cucumber
1 myoga ginger (ginger bud)
½ ounce (15g) broccoli
⅛ ounce (5g) cilantro (coriander), plus more for garnish
2 tablespoons Ceviche Sauce (see page 243)

1　Prepare the vegetables: thinly slice the red onion; cut the okra lengthways into three pieces. Cut each tomato into 6 pieces; dice the cucumber. Thinly slice the myoga ginger lengthways. Cook the broccoli in salted water until just tender, drain and refresh in iced water, then cut into bite-sized pieces. Finely chop the cilantro (coriander).
2　Put all the vegetables in a bowl and combine well with the Ceviche Sauce.
3　Transfer to serving dishes, arranging the various colors artfully, and top with more cilantro.

NOBU'S NOTE
•　This may be made with most seasonal vegetables.

サーモンケルプ　ロール
Salmon Kelp Roll

Pairing well-matched ingredients together enables the creation of complex combinations of taste and texture.

serves 2
½ sheet Shiroita Konbu kelp (5 x 8 inch/12 x 20cm)
2 ounces (60g) boneless skinless salmon fillet
2 large shiso leaves
1 garlic clove, cut into 6 thin slices
1 stick yamagobo root, rolled and cut into slices about ½ inch (1cm) thick
⅓ ounce (10g) scallions (spring onions), chopped
daikon for garnish
2 tablespoons ponzu (see page 63)
1 head of an edible flower
　　AMA-ZU (SWEET VINEGAR)
　　2 tablespoons rice vinegar
　　6 tablespoons granulated sugar
　　2½ teaspoons sea salt

1　Make the ama-zu by putting all the ingredients in a pan and warming through gently until the sugar dissolves.
2　Prepare the kelp: heat the ama-zu in a pan until it is just about to boil (it should not reach boiling point), then add the kelp. Simmer gently for 1 minute, remove the pan from the heat and leave it to cool at room temperature.
3　Peel off the skin of the salmon and cut the flesh into 6 thin slices about ⅛ inch (5mm) thick.
4　Drain the kelp well and spread it out on a sheet of plastic wrap. Place 4 salmon slices side by side and then the other 2 slices across them side by side.
5　Over the salmon slices, arrange the 2 large shiso leaves, the slices of garlic, yamagobo and scallions (spring onions). Roll up the kelp tightly into a cylinder.
6　Cut the roll across into 6 pieces and arrange them on a serving dish with daikon garnish in the middle. Pour some ponzu around the pieces and place the flower on the daikon.

オイスターシュターとウニシューター
Oyster and Sea Urchin Shooter

This can serve as a substitute for an aperitif in anticipation of the dishes to follow.

serves 2

1 fresh oyster

⅔ ounce (20g) sea urchin
  (5 to 6 small firm pieces)

2 quail eggs

momiji-oroshi

chopped scallion (spring onion)

2 teaspoons saké (Hokusetsu)

2 tablespoons ponzu (see page 63)

1　Extract the oyster from the shell. Prepare 2 large shot glasses and put the oyster in one and the sea urchin in the other.

2　Into each of the glasses, put some momiji-oroshi and scallion (spring onion), and then pour over that the saké and ponzu.

3　Crack one of the eggs into each glass.

4　To appreciate the full effect of the shooters, knock them back in one go.

NOBU'S NOTES

• Needless to say, the oyster and sea urchin must be very fresh.

• It is a good idea to crack the eggs into a cup or on to a plate first to check that they too are quite fresh.

h
o
appetizers

姫サザエのエスカルゴ風バターソース
Baby Turban Shells with Escargot Butter Sauce
The sauce used here for these sea snails is an adaptation of the classic French stuffing for escargots.

serves 3
6 baby turban shells
a little soy sauce
1 sudachi citrus fruit
ESCARGOT-STYLE BUTTER SAUCE
3½ ounces (100g) butter
1 ounce (30g) shallot, finely chopped
1 garlic clove, finely chopped
1 ounce (30g) parsley, finely chopped
1 teaspoon freshly squeezed lemon juice
a little sea salt

1   To make the Escargot-style butter sauce: soften the butter in a bowl by warming the bowl in hot water. Mix the butter and all the other sauce ingredients in the bowl, and season to taste with salt. Put the mixture in a circular mold and chill in the refrigerator to set.

2   Preheat the oven to 400°F (200°C, gas 6). Scrub the baby turban shells well under running water using a scourer. Cook in boiling well-salted water for about 2 minutes.

3   Open the shell and take out the meat. Cut off the guts, and put the meat back into the shell with the butter sauce. Add a drop of soy sauce and bake in the oven for about 5 minutes.

4   Shape piles of salt on a dish and place the turban shells on top. Arrange the halved sudachi citrus fruit beside the shells and put cocktail sticks on top for extracting the meat.

NOBU'S NOTES
*   When baking the shells, crumpled foil underneath the shells helps stabilize them.
*   To make the salt base for presentation, you can mix the salt with a little egg white and then shape this in a mold.
*   When first extracting the meat from the shell, use a skewer to pierce the top part of the meat and take it out while turning the shell, so as to be sure to extract all the innards without cutting them off.

姫ホタテ貝のパルメザンチーズ焼き
Parmesan Baked Small Scallops
The flavor of Parmesan cheese complements the sweetness of scallops very well.

serves 5
10 queen scallops
⅓ ounce (10g) butter
soy sauce
garlic, grated
parsley, finely chopped
10 teaspoons grated Parmesan cheese
1 lemon

1   Preheat the oven to 400°F (200°C, gas 6). Scrub the shells of the baby scallops and, using a knife, extract the scallops from their shells. Remove and discard the beard and the frilly outer membrane, and place the scallops back in the shells.

2   Over each scallop, place in turn: one-tenth of the butter, a drop of soy sauce, a little grated garlic and chopped parsley and 1 teaspoon of Parmesan cheese. Bake in the preheated oven for about 5 minutes.

3   While still hot, place the scallops in their shells on a dish, and serve with lemon cut across into thick slices.

NOBU'S NOTE
*   As with most shells, the scallops tend to move around on the plate, so it would be a good idea to serve them on a bed of salt as on pages 32–3.

小柱の串焼きと野菜のサルサ
Baby Scallop Skewers with Vegetable Salsa

白海老串揚げ

Minced Baby White Shrimp Skewers

This ensemble of white shrimp, scallop and fresh aonori laver is served with mayonnaise imbued with the refreshing flavor of fresh wasabi.

serves 3
2½ ounces (75g) raw shrimp (prawns) in the shell
1¼ ounces (35g) scallops in the shell
½ ounce (15g) fresh aonori
vegetable oil for deep-frying
4¼ ounces (120g) mayonnaise
¾ ounce (25g) fresh wasabi
chives
2 sudachi citrus fruit

1　Remove the heads, shell and tails from the shrimp (prawns); extract the scallops from their shells and remove the beard and innards. Cut the shrimp (prawns) and scallops into fairly small pieces, combining them on the board while chopping.
2　Mix the fresh aonori laver into the shrimp and scallops, and mold the mixture around 6-8 bamboo skewers.
3　Heat the oil for deep-frying to a temperature of 180°C (355°F) and deep-fry the skewers for 2 minutes. Drain on paper towel.
4　Combine the mayonnaise with the freshly grated wasabi. Spoon this into a small glass pot and sprinkle the chives on top. Serve with the sudachi citrus fruit.

温かいセビーチェ
Hot Ceviche

This very fashionable treatment for seafood, actually a basic of traditional good home cooking in Peru, is here revamped in Nobu style. To make this hot ceviche you will need two well-scrubbed stones each about the size of a fist, which are heated in the oven beforehand.

serves 4

4 kuruma shrimp (tiger prawns)
2 scallops
½ mongo cuttlefish
¼ red onion
2 red cherry tomatoes
2 yellow cherry tomatoes
½ cucumber
⅓ ounce (10g) cilantro (coriander), finely chopped, plus more for garnish
8 fluid ounces (225ml) dashi (see page 97)

CEVICHE SAUCE
2 teaspoons aji amarillo (orange chili paste, see page 242)
4 fluid ounces (120ml) freshly squeezed lemon juice
1 tablespoon and 1 teaspoon freshly squeezed yuzu juice
2 teaspoons soy sauce
¹⁄₁₂ ounce (2.5g) black pepper
⅓ ounce (10g) finely chopped garlic
⅛ ounce (5g) grated ginger
1 tablespoon plus 1 teaspoon well salted water (see page 62)

1   Preheat the oven to its highest setting and put the stones (see the introduction above) in there to get really hot.

2   Remove the heads and shells of the shrimp (prawns), leaving their tails on. Then devein them by cutting into their backs with a knife. Prepare the scallops as described on page 44 and halve them horizontally. Cut the body of the cuttlefish into 2 x 1¼ inch (5 x 2cm) strips. Score some fine lengthways incisions on the surface of each strip.

3   Thinly slice the red onion and halve the tomatoes. Slice the cucumber at an angle and finely chop the cilantro (coriander).

4   To make the Ceviche Sauce, put all the ingredients into a mixing bowl and mix well. The sauce is ready when the aji amarillo has dissolved and the sauce has turned yellow.

5   Mix 8 fluid ounces (225ml) of this sauce with the dashi and put in an earthenware pot together with the prepared ingredients.

6   Using gloves or tongs, put the hot stones into the pot and immediately cover with the lid. When the foaming has subsided, take out the stones.

7   Arrange all the ingredients, together with the sauce, attractively in a medium bowl and sprinkle the cilantro (coriander) garnish on top.

NOBU'S NOTE
• For ceviche, the South American dish of fish and shellfish "cooked" in a citrus dressing, you obviously need to have the very freshest of ingredients.

車海老とアスパラガス黄身ソース
キャビア添え
Shrimp and Asparagus with Egg Sauce

This assemblage of green asparagus, shrimp and caviar floating
in egg sauce makes a wonderfully colorful display.

serves 2

2 kuruma shrimp (tiger prawns), each about 1 ounce (30g)

vegetable oil for deep-frying

5 green asparagus spears

a little sea salt

⅓ ounce (10g) caviar

EGG SAUCE

1 egg yolk

1 tablespoon freshly squeezed lemon juice

a little soy sauce

1 tablespoon clarified butter

1   First prepare the egg sauce: put the egg yolk into a mixing
bowl, mix it with the lemon juice and soy sauce until well
combined, and then quickly mix in the clarified butter (see
below) to produce a thick sauce.

2   Pierce a wooden skewer through the shrimp (prawns),
starting from their mouths through to the tails, keeping the tails
straight. Cook in well-salted boiling water just until they turn
pink and then plunge into iced water to chill. Shell and cut off
their heads and tails, reserving the tails for garnish.

3   Heat the oil for deep-frying to a temperature of 180°C
(355°F). Peel the hard skin off the asparagus and deep-fry the
spears in the oil for 1 minute only. Drain and sprinkle a little sea
salt on the asparagus spears.

4   Line a serving dish with the sauce. Arrange the asparagus
spears side by side and place the shrimp (prawns) across the
spears. Top with the caviar and decorate with the reserved tails.

NOBU'S NOTE

*   When making the egg sauce, clarified butter will separate if
it is mixed slowly. Mix it in quickly with a whisk or a spoon,
so that the sauce is instantly emulsified.

揚げトロのスパイシーガーリックソース
Deep-fried Toro Tataki with Spicy Garlic Sauce

Here good-quality toro is deep-fried briefly and then paired with
the kick of the spicy garlic sauce.

serves 2

2 pieces of myoga ginger

2 fava (broad) bean pods

vegetable oil for deep-frying

a little sea salt

a little black pepper

3½ ounces (100g) boneless skinless toro (tuna belly) fillet

SPICY GARLIC SAUCE

3 tablespoons plus 1 teaspoon saké

1 tablespoon plus 1½ teaspoons soy sauce

3 fluid ounces (100ml) dashi (see page 97)

⅓ tablespoon chili garlic sauce

½ teaspoon grated garlic

½ teaspoon black pepper

3 tablespoons plus 1 teaspoon kuzu powder
dissolved in 6 tablespoons plus 2 teaspoons water

1   Cut the ginger into very thin strips. Cook the fava (broad)
beans in boiling salted water until just tender and remove the
skins.

2   Make the spicy garlic sauce: put all the ingredients except
the kuzu into a pan and bring to the boil. Add the kuzu
dissolved in water to thicken the sauce (see page 243).

3   Heat the oil for deep-frying to a temperature of 180°C
(355°F). Sprinkle the sea salt and black pepper over the toro fillet
and deep-fry in the hot oil for about 30 seconds. Plunge the
toro into iced water to cool it quickly and pat dry with paper
towel.

4   Cut the fillet into slices about ½ inch (1cm) thick, and
arrange the slices on a serving plate lined with the spicy garlic
sauce. Top with the thinly sliced ginger and the fava (broad)
beans.

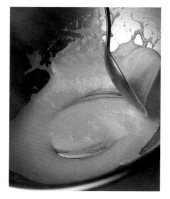

車海老とアスパラガス黄身ソース　キャビア添え
Shrimp and Asparagus with Egg Sauce

揚げトロのスパイシーガーリックソース
Deep-fried Toro Tataki with Spicy Garlic Sauce

車海老の春巻
Kuruma Shrimp Roll

The firm texture of kuruma shrimp (tiger prawn) is
complemented by caviar and salsa.

serves 1

1 kuruma shrimp (tiger prawn), about 1½ ounces (40g)

½ shiitake mushroom

1 large shiso leaf

1 endive (chicory) leaf

¼ sheet pâte brique

a little yuzu pepper

vegetable oil for deep-frying

2 tablespoons Maui Onion Salsa (page 247)

1 teaspoon caviar

cilantro (coriander)

1   Remove the shell, head and tail of the shrimp (prawn). Cut
into the back of the shrimp with a knife, devein and slice
through the meat lengthwise.

2   Cut the mushroom into ¼ inch (5mm) slices. Cut the shiso
leaf in half and the endive (chicory) leaf into four.

3   Place on the sheet of pâte brique the halved shrimp (prawn)
pieces, alternating the heads and tails. Put the shiitake pieces on
top and sprinkle with the yuzu pepper. Spread the halved shiso
leaves over them and fold each side of the pastry over the filling,
then roll up away from you.

4   Heat the oil for deep-frying to a temperature of 180°C
(355°F). Deep-fry the roll in the hot oil until golden brown. Drain
on paper towel.

5   Spoon the Maui Onion Salsa into a cocktail glass and place
in it the endive (chicory) leaf and then the fried roll. Top with the
caviar and cilantro (coriander).

NOBU'S NOTE

• Eat the first bite of the roll with the caviar and then the
second bite onwards with the salsa.

salad

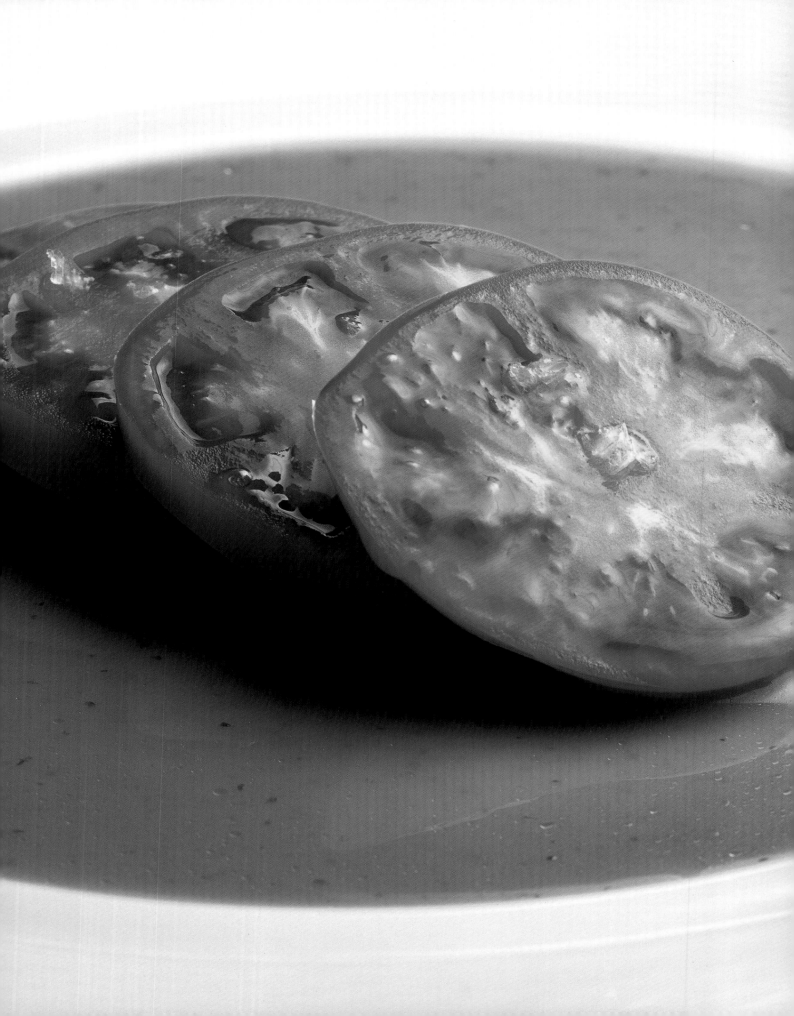

スズキとほうれん草のサラダ
Baby Spinach Salad with Sea Bass

活きダコとモロヘイヤのサラダ
Octopus and Molokheiya Salad

マグロの刺身サラダ　マツヒサドレッシング
Tuna Tataki Sashimi Salad with Matsuhisa Dressing

活きダコとモロヘイヤのサラダ
Octopus and Molokheiya Salad

The light sweetish flavor of raw octopus and the unique taste of molokheiya (Egyptian spinach) are matched by the Jalapeño Dressing.

serves 2

2 ounces (60g) North Pacific octopus, cut into 6 slices, each
  weighing about ⅓ ounce (10g)
1 bunch molokheiya (Egyptian spinach)
2 tablespoons Jalapeño Dressing (see page 246)
bonito flakes

1   Remove the skin of the octopus. Knead the skin and the suckers on the tentacles with salt in a ceramic mortar. Rinse off the salt. Knead the skin and suckers again to remove the slime and then rinse again. Repeat this process until the foam stops coming out.

2   Cook the skin and suckers in boiling water for about 1 minute. Cut the suckers off the skin and reserve for decoration.

3   Cut the octopus tentacles into very thin slices, about ¹⁄₁₆ in (1mm) thick. Cut off the root of the suckers, in order to stabilize them when they are used for decoration later on.

4   Strip the molokheiya leaves and mound them into the middle of a serving dish. Place the octopus slices around them and put a sucker on each slice. Pour the Jalapeño Dressing around the octopus and garnish with bonito flakes.

NOBU'S NOTE

• When the raw octopus is cut into thin slices, the slices curl up, adding to the attractiveness of the presentation.

マグロの刺身サラダ
マツヒサドレッシング
Tuna Tataki Sashimi Salad
with Matsuhisa Dressing

Sashimi salad makes the vegetables even more appetizing. Cut the tuna very thinly to create a texture balance.

serves 4

4¼ ounces (120g) boneless skinless tuna fillet
sea salt
black pepper
a little grapeseed or olive oil

SLICED SALAD
2 cucumbers
2 baby daikon
½ endive (chicory)
½ red endive (treviso)
1 celery stalk
2 radishes
1 asparagus spear
1 small turnip
2 myoga ginger (ginger bud)
1¾ ounces (50g) lotus root
3 tablespoons plus 1 teaspoon Matsuhisa Dressing
  (see page 247)
watercress

1   Sprinkle the tuna with salt and pepper and press these into the fillet. Briefly sear both sides of the tuna in a little oil. When the surface has just started to cook and appears marbled, plunge the fillet into iced water to cool, then pat with paper towel until completely dry.

2   For the sliced salad, shave the vegetables extremely thinly with a vegetable slicer and leave in iced water. When the vegetables are crisp, drain in a sieve. Mix the vegetables and make a heap in the center of a serving plate.

3   Cut the tuna fillet into 7 slices about ⅛ inch (3mm) thick and roll each slice into a cylinder. Arrange the tuna rolls around the vegetables and pour the Matsuhisa Dressing on top. Garnish with watercress.

NOBU'S NOTE

• When slicing the vegetables, cut them lengthways to show the vegetable's natural shape. For example, slice cucumber, celery and ginger along the fibers.

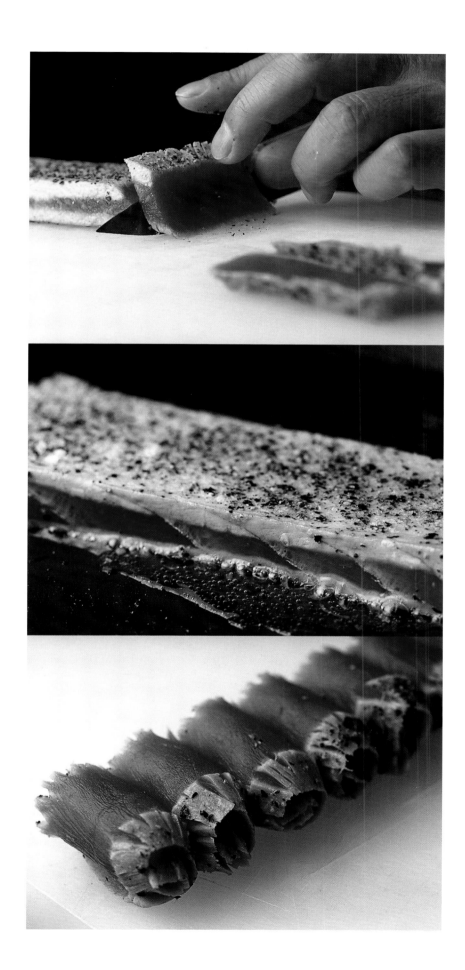

クレソンとホワイトアスパラガスのサラダ
クレソンドレッシング和え
Watercress and White Asparagus Salad with Watercress Dressing

This is a dish that makes the most of watercress and white asparagus. The amounts given make quite generous servings.

serves 2

2 bunches watercress

5 spears white asparagus

milk

1 udo

WATERCRESS DRESSING:

2 teaspoons sea salt

½ tablespoon freshly ground black pepper, coarsely ground

3½ fluid ounces (100ml) rice vinegar

3 tablespoons plus 1 teaspoon grapeseed oil

black sesame seeds

1   Chop the watercress and separate into thick stalks and thinner stalks with leaves. Briefly blanch the thick stalks which will be used for the watercress dressing in a pan of boiling water. Refresh in iced water and drain.

2   Peel off the hard fibers from the asparagus spears, then put them in simmering milk, turn off the heat and leave them to cool in the milk for about 10 minutes. Briefly put them in iced water. Drain them and pat dry with paper towel. Cut the asparagus spears into bite-sized lengths.

3   Peel the udo into a thin unbroken strip, cut the strip at an oblique angle, wind the strips around a rod and place them in iced water to make udo curls.

4   Make the Watercress Dressing: combine 2 ounces (60g) of the blanched thick watercress stalks with the rest of the dressing ingredients in a mixer.

5   Arrange the white asparagus and the udo curls on a serving dish and heap the thin watercress stalks and leaves on the asparagus. Taking account of the color combination, pour the dressing where it would look most attractive. Serve with black sesame seeds sprinkled over the watercress.

NOBU'S NOTE

•   An important feature of white asparagus is its crunchy texture, so make sure that it is not cooked too long in the milk.

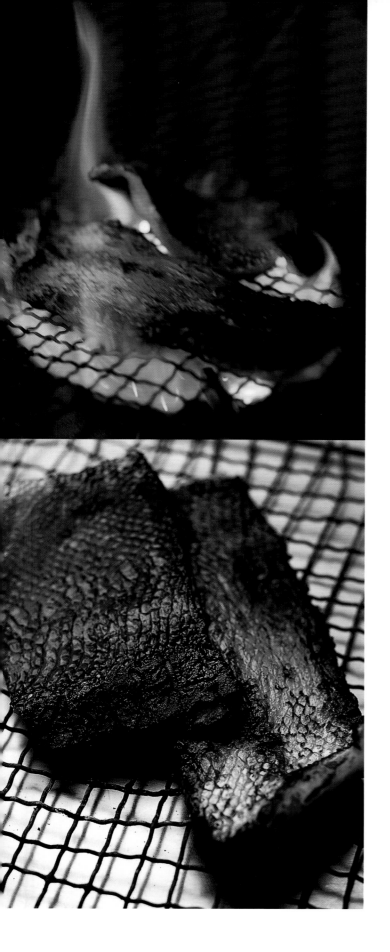

サーモンスキンサラダ
Salmon Skin Salad

Crisp and savory salmon skin, daikon and kaiware daikon here create a special harmony of flavor and texture.

serves 2

3 ounces (85g) smoked salmon skin

⅕ daikon

2 packs kaiware daikon (daikon shoots)

3 tablespoons Tosazu Vinegar and Soy Sauce (see page 244)

1 tablespoon freshly squeezed yuzu juice

white sesame seeds, roasted in a dry pan

bonito flakes

1   Grill the salmon skin on a hot griddle until crisp. Cut the skin into strips, about ¼ inch (8mm) wide.

2   Peel the daikon into a thin unbroken strip and cut the strip into 4 sheets, about 6 inches (15cm) long. Put the 4 sheets together and cut them into strips about ⅛ inch (3mm) wide. Plunge the strips into water until crisp. Drain. Cut off and discard the roots of the kaiware daikon; rinse and drain in a sieve.

3   Combine the salmon skin and vegetables in a mixing bowl and mix with the Tosazu Vinegar and Soy Sauce and the yuzu juice.

4   Transfer the salad to a serving bowl, sprinkle with freshly roasted white sesame seeds, and top with the bonito flakes.

NOBU'S NOTE

• Grilling the salmon skin reduces the fattiness and produces a savory crisp texture. If necessary, it can be seared on a hob that has a metal grid.

sas
h
imi

タイの刺身とドライ味噌
Snapper Sashimi with Dried Miso

Dried miso has an unexpectedly intense flavor and adds a kick to the delicately flavored snapper.

serves 4

1 garlic clove

vegetable oil for frying

5½ ounces (160g) boneless skinless red snapper fillet, cut into 16 slices about ⅛ inch
  (3mm) thick and weighing about ⅓ ounce (10g)

1 tablespoon extra virgin olive oil

⅓ ounce (10g) scallion (spring onion), thinly sliced

DRIED MISO
  3½ ounces (100g) white miso

1   To prepare the dried miso: thinly spread the white miso on a sheet of cooking paper and dry in the sun for 1 day. Peel the miso from the paper, break it into pieces and mix in a food processor until it becomes granular.

2   Slice the garlic and fry in the oil (at about 285–300°F/140–150°C) until nicely colored to make garlic chips.

3   Fan out the snapper slices on a serving dish and sprinkle evenly over them the dried miso (about 2 tablespoons). Drizzle the extra virgin olive oil over the top, place the garlic chips in the middle, and garnish with the sliced scallion (spring onion).

NOBU'S NOTE
•   If the miso can't be dried in the sun, it can be baked in an oven at its lowest possible setting for about 24 hours.

オイスター・ティラディート
Oyster Tiradito

神戸牛　ニュースタイルサシミ
Kobe Beef New-Style Sashimi

ソフトシェルクラブの唐揚　カクタスリーフのサルサ
Deep-fried Soft Shell Crab with Cactus Salsa

ソフトシェルクラブの春巻
Soft Shell Crab Spring Roll

ソフトシェルクラブの唐揚
カクタスリーフのサルサ
Deep-fried Soft Shell Crab with Cactus Salsa

This dish of soft shell crab is given a novel twist by the addition of a piquant cactus salsa.

serves 2
vegetable oil for deep-frying
1 soft shell crab
arrowroot

> CACTUS LEAF SALSA
> *1³⁄₄ ounces (50g) edible cactus leaves*
> *½ cucumber*
> *¼ red onion*
> *½ red chilli*
> *2 tablespoons Ceviche Sauce (see page 243)*

1   Heat oil for deep-frying to a temperature of 355°F (180°C). Dust the soft shell crab with arrowroot and deep-fry in the hot oil for 4 to 5 minutes. Drain.
2   Skin the cactus leaves and cut into ¼ inch (5mm) cubes. Plunge the cubes into boiling water, then immediately chill in iced water and pat dry with a paper towel. Chop the cucumber and red onions into cubes that are the same size as the cactus pieces. Slice the red chilli into thin circles.
3   To make the cactus leaf salsa: put the cactus, cucumber, onion and chili into a mixing bowl and combine with the Ceviche Sauce.
4   Deep-fry the crab again for 1 minute to crisp it up. Drain well, cut it into bite-size pieces and arrange on a serving dish. Serve with the cactus leaf salsa in a small separate bowl. (Alternatively, spoon the salsa over the soft shell crab just before serving.)

NOBU'S NOTE
•   To create the cactus cubes, first cut the cactus into 2-inch (5cm) strips. After skinning, cut the strips into thinner strips, then cut these across at right angles to create cubes.

ソフトシェルクラブの春巻
Soft Shell Crab Spring Roll

This dish has been created to give the flavor of the increasingly popular soft shell crab more complexity.

serves 2
vegetable oil for deep-frying
1 soft shell crab
arrowroot
2 scallops
10 shrimp (prawns)
¼ red pepper
2 shiitake mushrooms
²⁄₃ ounce (20g) leek
1 large shiso leaf
a little light soy sauce
a little saké
a little sea salt
1 sheet egg (spring) roll wrapper
udo
thick balsamic vinegar
lamb's lettuce

> WASABI MAYONNAISE
> *4¼ ounces (120g) mayonnaise*
> *¾ ounce (25g) wasabi paste*

1   Heat oil for deep-frying to a temperature of 355°F (180°C). Dust the soft shell crab with arrowroot and deep-fry in the hot oil for 4 to 5 minutes. Drain well and cut into 4 pieces.
2   Finely chop together the scallops and the shrimp (prawns). Cut the red pepper into thin strips, soak in water and wipe dry.
3   Chop the shiitake mushrooms and leeks and deep-fry without dusting with flour until crisp. Drain well.
4   Put the shrimp, pepper, mushrooms and leeks in a mixing bowl. Add the soy sauce, saké, and sea salt, and mix well.
5   Lay the shiso leaf on the egg (spring) roll wrapper and spread the mixture over the pastry. Place on top of this the quartered soft shell crab pieces, fold each side of the pastry sheet over the filling, then roll up away from you.
6   Again heat oil for deep-frying to a temperature of 355°F (180°C).Deep-fry the roll in the hot oil for 3 to 4 minutes and drain.
7   Make the wasabi mayonnaise by mixing the ingredients.
8   Place the curled udo in the middle of a serving plate. Cut the roll into bite-size pieces and arrange them to stand on the wasabi mayonnaise. Pour the balsamic vinegar on to four places on the plate. Top the udo curls with the lamb's lettuce.

NOBU'S NOTE
•   When deep-frying the roll, pay attention to the color and lift out the roll when it turns golden brown.

タラバ蟹のツメの天婦羅
バターポン酢ソース

King Crab Claw Tempura with Butter Ponzu Sauce

serves 2

2 king crab claws
vegetable oil for deep-frying
flour
2 shiitake mushrooms
½ small eggplant (aubergine)
a little shichimi togarashi

> TEMPURA BATTER
> *1 egg yolk*
> *6¾ fluid ounces (200ml) iced water*
> *3½ ounces (100g) all-purpose (plain) flour*
>
> SIMPLE BUTTER PONZU SAUCE
> *4 tablespoons ponzu (see page 63)*
> *1 tablespoon melted clarified butter*

1   Make the tempura batter by lightly mixing the ingredients.
2   Blanch the crab claws briefly if raw and remove the shells except for the tips of the claws.
3   Heat oil for deep-frying to 355°F (180°C). Dust the crab claws lightly with flour, dip in the batter and fry in the hot oil for about 2 minutes. Drain well on paper towel.
4   Remove the stems from the shiitake, make shallow incisions on the tops to create star shapes for decoration. Flour and dip in the batter. Deep-fry until crisp. Drain well on paper towel.
5   Cut the eggplant (aubergine) into 3 or 4 oval sections. Slice each piece from one end in a series of not quite parallel cuts, leaving it joined at that end, then fan it out slightly. Flour and dip in batter, then deep-fry until crisp. Drain well.
6   Make the simple butter ponzu sauce by mixing the clarified butter into the ponzu. Sprinkle with shichimi togarashi and serve the tempura immediately with the sauce for dipping.

NOBU'S NOTE
• Butter ponzu sauce needs to be served immediately because the fat will separate when it cools down.

タラバ蟹の天婦羅　甘酢ポン酢

King Crab Tempura with Sweet and Sour Ponzu Sauce

King crab is not very juicy or succulent, but its flavor can be greatly enhanced when served as tempura.

serves 2

3 king crab legs
vegetable oil for deep-frying
flour
tempura batter (see left)
¼ red onion
⅙ ounce (5g) jalapeño chili

> AMA-ZU PONZU SAUCE:
> *2 tablespoons plus 2 teaspoons ama-zu (see page 36)*
> *2 teaspoons ponzu (see page 63)*

1   Cut and separate the king crab legs at their joints. Take each piece with the softer side (white side) of the shell facing up and trim off their shells with a knife to extract the meat. Cut off both ends of the meat to make the pieces all of the same length.
2   Heat oil for deep-frying to a temperature of 355°F (180°C). Dust the pieces of crab meat lightly with flour, dip them in the tempura batter and deep-fry in the hot oil for 2 to 3 minutes until the batter is crisp. Drain on paper towels.
3   Thinly slice the red onions. Chop the jalapeño into thin pieces.
4   Arrange the fried crab legs on a serving dish and sprinkle with the red onion and jalapeño. Make the Ama-zu Ponzu Sauce by mixing the ingredients together and spoon this around the tempura.

NOBU'S NOTES
• Ama-zu Ponzu Sauce can be poured over the crab legs. When you do so, serve the dish quickly so that the crispiness of the tempura batter is not lost.
• Do not overmix tempura batter or it will become heavy; it is best if there are a few lumps of flour left visible in the mix.

タラバ蟹のツメの天婦羅　バターポン酢ソース
King Crab Claw Tempura with Butter Ponzu Sauce

タラバ蟹の天婦羅　甘酢ポン酢
King Crab Tempura with Sweet and Sour Ponzu Sauce

ロックシュリンプの天婦羅　クリーミースパイシーソース
Rock Shrimp Tempura with Creamy Spicy Sauce

オイスター・フィロー
Oyster Filo

Transform raw oysters into a sumptuous fried dish – a Nobu-style way with them is to wrap them in filo pastry before deep-frying them.

serves 1

1 oyster

flour

Tempura Batter (see page 103)

1 ounce (30g) shredded filo pastry

vegetable oil for deep-frying

1 large salad leaf

a little finely shredded red cabbage for garnish

VEGETABLE SAUCE

7½ ounces (220g) tomato, grated

3½ ounces (100g) apples, grated

4½ ounces (120g) caster sugar

3 tablespoons plus 1 teaspoon rice vinegar

1 tablespoon plus 2 teaspoons soy sauce

⅛ ounce (5g) black pepper

⅝ ounce (17.5g) cornstarch (cornflour)

about 4⅛-5¼ fluid ounces (130-150ml) water

⅙ ounce (5g) onion, grated

a little garlic, grated

pinch of salt

2 teaspoons granulated sugar, cooked to a caramel with

1 tablespoon water

WASABI MAYONNAISE

4½ ounces (120g) mayonnaise

¾ ounce (25g) wasabi paste

1   First make the vegetable sauce: put all the ingredients in a saucepan and cook over medium heat. As the mixture will gradually thicken because of the cornstarch (cornflour), stir constantly while heating and turn off the heat immediately before the mixture comes to a boil. Strain the mixture using a straining cloth and put in a sterilized airtight jar or container. If necessary, make up to 18 fluid ounces (500ml) with some more water. When the sauce has cooled down, put a lid on it and it will keep in the refrigerator for up to a week.

2   Extract the oyster from its shell and rinse under running water.

3   Heat oil for deep-frying to a temperature of 340°F (170°C). Dust the oyster lightly with flour and dip in the tempura batter. Unravel the shredded filo and spread it out. Place the batter-coated oyster at the edge of the filo, then roll up away from you about 3 to 4 times. Adjust the direction of rolling so that a neat round shape is formed.

4   Deep-fry the filo-wrapped oyster in the hot oil for about 3 minutes and drain on paper towels.

5   Make the Wasabi Mayonnaise by mixing the mayonnaise and wasabi.

6   Line a serving plate with a salad leaf and drizzle over it the Wasabi Mayonnaise. Place the oyster filo on top and pour over some of the vegetable sauce. Garnish with red cabbage strips.

NOBU'S NOTES

*   Use grated daikon to remove dirt and debris from the extracted oyster meat. In that way, the oyster meat will stay firm.
*   When frying, rotate the oyster filo in the oil to wrap the shreds of filo around the oyster.
*   When eating, wrap the oyster filo with the salad leaf.

オイスター・フィロー

アワビの天婦羅
Abalone Tempura

アワビの天婦羅
Abalone Tempura

In order to preserve the firm and springy texture of the abalone, fry it only briefly and then serve immediately.

serves 4

1 abalone in the shell, about 18 ounces (500g)

vegetable oil for deep-frying

flour

tempura batter (see page 103)

handful wasabi leaves

1 sudachi citrus fruit

Japanese maple sprigs for garnish

CURRY SALT

¼ tablespoon curry powder

1 tablespoon sea salt

1   Prepare the abalone in its shell: in order not to damage the abalone meat, use a wooden spatula to extract it from its shell. Wash it under running water, using a brush to remove dirt and debris. Cut the abalone meat into thin slices, about 1/16 inch (2mm) thick. Use a knife to score a fine criss-cross of incisions on the surface of abalone.

2   Heat oil for deep-frying to a temperature of 355°F (180°C). Pat the abalone slices dry with paper towel and dust lightly with flour. Dip each into the tempura batter and deep-fry in the hot oil for about 1 minute.

3   Line a serving dish with a sheet of paper and then place wasabi leaves on top. Arrange the abalone tempura to form an attractive pile.

4   Make the curry salt by mixing the curry powder and sea salt, and put into a small bowl. Slice the top and the bottom off the sudachi citrus fruit, cut it into 2 halves and put one on top of the other.

5   Place both the curry salt and the sudachi beside the abalone tempura. Garnish the dish with a Japanese maple sprig with green leaves.

NOBU'S NOTE

•   It is important not to coat the abalone too thickly in the tempura batter.

ウニととうもろこしのかきあげ
Sea Urchin and Corn Khakiage

The sweetness of sea urchin coated in tempura batter floods the palate.

serves 2

vegetable oil for deep-frying

2 ounces (60g) baby corn

⅔ ounce (20g) scallions (spring onions)

4¼ ounces (120g) sea urchin

2 tablespoons plus 1 teaspoon Tempura Batter (see page 103)

sea salt

coarsely ground black pepper

½ sudachi citrus fruit

freshly squeezed lemon juice

1   Heat oil for deep-frying to a temperature of 355°F (180°C). Cut the baby corn lengthways into long pieces. Cut the scallions (spring onions) to the same length. Put them together with the sea urchin in a mixing bowl and mix with the tempura batter.

2   Put one bite-size amount of the mixture at a time into the hot oil and fry for 2 to 3 minutes.

3   Line a serving dish with a sheet of paper and arrange the well-drained khakiage on it.

4   Serve with sea salt, coarsely ground pepper, sudachi citrus fruit and freshly squeezed lemon juice.

NOBU'S NOTE

•   When mixing the ingredients with the batter, handle them carefully so as not to crush the sea urchin.

アワビの天婦羅

ウニととうもろこしのかきあげ
Sea Urchin and Corn Khakiage

穴子のFish & Chips
Sea Eel 'Fish & Chips'

118

ウニとかぶらの蒸しもの
Sea Urchin Pudding

In this steamed dish the savory flavors of produce from the land and the sea are lightly enveloped in gin'an. Delicate emphasis is given to the natural sweetness of the sea urchin and turnip.

serves 3

2 small turnips

2 egg whites

½ teaspoon sea salt

4¼ ounces (120g) fresh sea urchin, plus 3 sea urchin shells

3 tablespoons gin'an (see page 127)

1   Grate the turnips and squeeze out the moisture. Beat the egg whites in a bowl until standing in stiff peaks. Mix in the grated turnip and season with sea salt.

2   Pile the sea urchin carefully into the cleaned shells, then spoon egg mixture around the sea urchin.

3   Place the urchin shells on some crumpled foil and cook for 7 to 8 minutes in a steamer over a medium heat. After steaming, carefully top with the gin'an.

4   Serve on a plate with the individual sea urchin shells placed on top of small piles of salt.

NOBU'S NOTE

• Use only fresh sea urchins that are still alive. Arrange the sea urchins so that they can be clearly seen inside the shells.

ウニとフカヒレの茶碗蒸し
Shark's Fin and Sea Urchin Pudding

This sumptuous offering of sea urchin and whole steamed shark's fin is bowl-steamed to develop the abundant yet delicate tastes of the sea.

serves 1

1 largish shark's fin
3½ fluid ounces (100ml) saké
small knob of ginger, unpeeled and thickly sliced
½ scallion (spring onion), green parts only, roughly chopped
⅓ ounce (10g) sea urchin
½ finger of okra

CHAWAN-MUSHI CUSTARD
10½ fluid ounces (300ml) dashi (see page 97)
1 egg
1¾ tablespoons saké
1¾ tablespoons light soy sauce
1 teaspoon sea salt

GIN'AN
6¾ fluid ounces (200ml) dashi (see page 97)
1 tablespoon sake
1 tablespoon light soy sauce
pinch of sea salt
kuzu or arrowroot

1   Place the shark's fin in a pan steamer together with the saké, ginger, and the onion. Steam over a high heat for about 1 hour.

2   To make the Chawan-mushi Custard: put the dashi into a bowl and add the egg. Season with the saké, soy sauce, and sea salt. Stir the mixture without causing it to froth. Strain through a fine cloth.

3   Put the sea urchin and the steamed shark's fin into a pan, carefully pour over the Chawan-mushi mixture, and steam for 15 minutes - the first 2 minutes over a medium heat, then turn the heat down to low. To finish, add the okra and gently heat through.

4   To make the Gin'an: warm the dashi, season with the soy sauce, then add the kuzu, mixed with about twice its volume of water, the sake and salt. Adjust the amount of water until you have a coating consistency.

5   When the Chawan-mushi Custard is ready, place it in the middle of the bowl and arrange the shark's fin around it in a graceful arc. Serve with the gin'an carefully poured over everything and the steamed okra on top of the custard.

NOBU'S NOTES
- If a froth forms on top of the egg custard while you are making it, mop it up with paper towel and discard.
- Be careful to regulate the heat under the Chawan-mushi. If it is too strong, the surface will be marked with small steam holes.

アボカドの茶碗蒸し
Avocado Egg Pudding

Popularly known as 'Californian chawan-mushi', this dish can be served warm or cold, depending on the season.

serves 1

3½ ounces (100g) avocado
6¾ fluid ounces (200ml) dashi (see page 97)
3½ fluid ounces (100ml) egg white
1 tablespoon saké
1 tablespoon light soy sauce
pinch of sea salt
4 shelled snow crab
½ cucumber
3 tablespoons gin'an (see page 127)

1   Halve the avocado, remove the stone and skin. Cut the avocado flesh roughly into cubes, then finely chop. Press the pieces of avocado flesh through a sieve to make a paste.

2   Place the avocado paste in a bowl. Mix in the dashi and egg white. Mix together the saké, soy sauce, and sea salt, and mix that with the avocado a little at a time. Using a spatula, gradually blend the ingredients. When they are well blended, pass the mixture through a sieve again.

3   Cut the snow crab into pieces about ⅜ inch (1cm) square; cut the cucumber into pieces about ⅛ inch (3mm) square.

4   Put the crab meat into a steamer, add the avocado mixture and steam for 15 to 20 minutes over a medium heat.

5   When serving the pudding hot, place the chopped cucumber on top, and then cover with warm gin'an. When serving it cold, allow the steamed mixture to cool and then chill in the refrigerator. Put the chopped cucumber on top just before serving, and cover with cold gin'an.

NOBU'S NOTES
*   If you add the avocado that is being sieved to the seasoning mixture a little at a time, it will tend to reduce any risk of congealing.
*   Ceramic bowls go well with warm puddings (decorated with an orchid leaf), and glass bowls with ice work well with cold puddings (with a striped bamboo leaf).

エイヒレ　スパイシーブラックビーンソース
Ray Fin with Spicy Black Bean Sauce

キンキの湯葉包み蒸し
Steamed Kinki Yuba Roll

Reconstituted dry-folded sardines enhanced with the flavor from the gin'an wonderfully complement the slightly oily kinki.

serves 2

2 sheets tatami-iwasi (dry-folded sardines)

2 kinki fillets

2 sheets Hiei yuba (soy milk skin)

sea salt

black pepper

2 tablespoons saké

6¾ fluid ounces (200ml) gin'an (see page 127)

a few cooked edamame

KOCHUJANG MISO

1 tablespoon kochujang (red pepper paste)

1 tablespoon Nobu-Style Saikyo Sweet Miso
  (see page 245)

1 teaspoon nikiri zaké or sake

1   Reconstitute the dry-folded sardines in fresh water overnight.

2   Make the Kochujang Miso by mixing together the ingredients.

3   Remove any bones from the stomach area and the darker flesh of the fish. Spread a sheet of yuba out, place a kinki fillet on the sheet and sprinkle with salt and pepper. Spread 2 tablespoons Kochujang Miso over the skin side. Start rolling the yuba from the side nearest you, sealing the ends as you would an egg (spring) roll. Make another roll in the same way .

4   Place the rolls in a suitable pan and sprinkle with saké. Cover with plastic wrap and steam over a high heat for 10 minutes.

5   Squeeze excess water out of the dry-folded sardines. Make the gin'an as described on page 127, but when the dashi comes to the boil, sprinkle the dry-folded sardines into it.

6   Place the steamed kinki wrapped in yuba on a plate. Pour over the gin'an and dry-folded sardine mixture, and finally sprinkle with the cooked edamame.

NOBU'S NOTE

• The flavor of the Kochujang Miso and dry-folded sardines goes really well with the slightly oily kinki. You might like to try using a few anchovies instead of the dry-folded sardines.

sau
té

フォアグラの味噌漬け焼き
Foie Gras with Miso

Here an essentially Japanese flavor is given to foie gras by pickling it in miso. The miso cuts through the richness of the foie gras, allowing you to savor the lighter taste.

serves 2

2 slices of foie gras, each about 1¾ ounces (50g)

flour

2 tablespoons grapeseed oil

a few sansho sprigs (kinome)

1 hajikami (pickled ginger shoot)

Yuzu Miso Sauce (see page 41) to taste

NOBU-STYLE SAIKYO MISO PICKLING MIXTURE

5¼ fluid ounces (150ml) saké

5¼ fluid ounces (150ml) mirin

1 pound (450g) white miso (Yamajirushi Sangiku)

8 ounces (225g) granulated sugar

1   The day before you want to serve, make the Nobu-Style Saikyo Miso Pickling Mixture: put the saké and mirin in a pan, bring to a boil, and boil to drive off the alcohol and reduce by about 10 per cent. Reduce to a medium heat and add the white miso paste, a little at a time. Blend with a wooden spatula. When you have added all the white miso paste and the mixture is smooth, turn the heat back up to high and stir in the sugar in two or three lots, making sure each has completely dissolved before adding any more. Make sure it does not burn. Remove from the heat and leave to cool to room temperature in a deep metal tray.

2   Once cool, pickle the foie gras slices in the miso mixture for a day.

3 Next day, preheat the oven to 400°F (200°C, gas 6). Remove the pickled foie gras from the mixture. Wipe off any miso and residual moisture on the foie gras, then lightly flour the pieces.

4   Heat the grapeseed oil in an ovenproof frying pan until very hot and sear the foie gras briefly on both sides.

5   When the outside of the foie gras is crisp and brown, place the frying pan with the foie gras in the preheated oven for 2 minutes.

6   Place a slice of foie gras in the middle of each of the serving plates. Press a few sansho sprigs between your hands to draw out their fragrance and place 5 or 6 shoots on each serving, then add the ginger. Serve with a little Yuzu Miso Sauce dotted around the foie gras.

NOBU'S NOTES

*   The Nobu-Style Saikyo Miso Pickling Mixture should be quite loose. When you put the foie gras into the mixture, make sure you cover it with the miso using a spatula or similar.
*   The pickling mixture can also be used for fish, including cod, mackerel, and yellowtail.
*   Do not overheat the foie gras – it should be served rare.

ハモとフォアグラ　和風トリュフソース
Hamo and Foie Gras with Japanese Truffle Sauce

ハモとフォアグラ　和風トリュフソース
Hamo and Foie Gras with Japanese Truffle Sauce

マグロのホホ肉　フカヒレブラックビーンソース
Tuna Cheek with Shark's Fin Black Bean Sauce

ハモとフォアグラ　和風トリュフソース
Hamo and Foie Gras with Japanese Truffle Sauce

Combining hamo, or conger eel, with foie gras makes an
unusually appetite-stimulating dish. Finishing it off with white
truffle oil gives the dish depth and body.

serves 2

3½ ounces (100g) boneless skinless hamo (conger eel) fillet

1¾ ounces (50g) foie gras

flour

3 tablespoons and 1 teaspoon saké

2 tablespoons mirin

2 teaspoons soy sauce

a little grapeseed oil

a little white truffle oil

3 long green sweet peppers

ground Japanese pepper

1　Cut the hamo fillet into bite-size pieces, thread on metal
skewers, and cook unseasoned under a hot broiler (grill) until
well colored and cooked through.

2　Dust the foie gras with flour using a brush.

3　Mix the saké, mirin, and soy sauce together in a cup.

4　Heat the grapeseed oil in a frying pan. When hot, place the
foie gras in the pan and lightly sear on both sides.

5　Move the foie gras to one side of the frying pan. Place the
broiled hamo in the space in the pan and add the sake mixture.
Continue to heat, coating the hamo with the sauce, until the
liquid becomes glossy. Finish by adding the white truffle oil.

6　Flash fry the peppers in a little more oil, then cut in half
lengthways.

7　Arrange the pepper halves on plates. Lay the hamo on top
of the peppers, the foie gras on top of the hamo, and sprinkle
with ground Japanese pepper.

NOBU'S NOTE

• Turn the hamo as you heat it through, coating it well with
the sauce. To avoid the foie gras overcooking, it can be
heated simply by placing it on top of the hamo.

マグロのホホ肉
フカヒレブラックビーンソース
Tuna Cheek with Shark's Fin Black Bean Sauce

This true symphony of flavors is composed of plump tuna cheek
with Shark's Fin Black Bean Sauce and Nobu-Style Saikyo Sweet
Miso.

serves 2

3 ounces (85g) tuna cheek

sea salt

black pepper

flour

grapeseed oil

red sweet pepper

asatsuki chives, cut into 2-inch (4cm) lengths

white part of scallions (spring onions), very finely sliced
lengthways

SHARK'S FIN BLACK BEAN SAUCE

1¾ ounces (50g) dried shark's fin, soaked in cold water
overnight

handful of chopped onion

knob of ginger, chopped

2 tablespoons Chinese shokoshu rice wine

6 fluid ounces (180ml) dashi (see page 97)

5 tablespoons plus 1 teaspoon saké

2 tablespoons plus 2 teaspoons mirin

2 tablespoons plus 2 teaspoons soy sauce

2 tablespoons Nobu-Style Saikyo Sweet Miso (see page 245)

1 tablespoon black bean paste

3 tablespoons kuzu powder, dissolved in a little water

1　Prepare the shark's fin for the sauce: place the drained
rehydrated shark's fin on a dish with the onion, ginger, rice
wine, dashi, and half the saké. Steam for about 40 minutes in a
steamer. Lay open carefully with chopsticks.

2　Preheat the oven to 475°F (250°C, gas 9). Season the tuna
cheeks and coat lightly with flour. Heat some grapeseed oil in an
ovenproof frying pan. Shake any excess flour from the tuna
cheeks and place them in the frying pan. Brown over a high
heat, remove and place the frying pan in the preheated oven for
about 3 minutes.

3　Make the Shark's Fin Black Bean Sauce. Combine the
remaining saké with the mirin, soy sauce, Nobu-Style Saikyo
Sweet Miso, and black bean paste in a pot and bring to the boil,
then add the prepared shark's fin. Bring to the boil again and
add the kuzu paste to thicken.

4　Place the tuna cheeks on plates, and pour over the shark's
fin black bean sauce. Then arrange a single lightly fried sweet
pepper and the chives on the cheeks. Finally pile on the scallion
(spring onion) whites.

NOBU'S NOTE

• The tuna cheeks look very appealing if they are seared with
red-hot skewers arranged in a criss-cross pattern.

車海老のガーリックオリーブオイル焼き
Garlic Sautéed Kuruma Shrimp

アジのソテーとスパイシーレモンドレッシング
Sautéed Horse Mackerel with Spicy Lemon Dressing

平目のホホ肉のディープフライ
ブラックペッパー　チリガーリック

Deep-fried Halibut Cheek with Black Pepper Chili Garlic Sauce

The pale but fatty halibut cheeks, known in Japanese as ohyo or ohirame, are deep-fried and served with a refreshingly piquant sauce.

serves 2
²/₃ ounce (20g) bamboo shoots
4 snowpeas (mangetouts)
4¼ ounces (120g) halibut cheeks
sea salt
black pepper
flour
katakuriko
vegetable oil for deep-frying
scallion (spring onion) whites, thinly sliced lengthways

BLACK PEPPER CHILI GARLIC SAUCE
1 tablespoon clarified butter
5¼ fluid ounces (150ml) dashi (see page 97)
½ tablespoon chili garlic sauce
2 tablespoons plus 1 teaspoon light soy sauce
5 tablespoons saké
1 teaspoon black pepper
1 teaspoon finely grated garlic
reconstituted kuzu

1   Cook the bamboo shoots and snowpeas (mangetouts) in boiling salted water until just tender. Refresh in cold water and drain well.

2   Make a cross-hatch of incisions on both sides of the halibut cheeks to let the heat penetrate them, then cut them into bite-size pieces. Season with salt and pepper. Dust with flour. Shake off excess and dredge with katakuriko.

3   Heat oil for deep-frying to a temperature of 355°F (180°C) and fry the halibut cheeks for 4 to 5 minutes until crisp on the outside. Drain well on paper towel.

4   Make the Black Pepper Chili Garlic Sauce: put the clarified butter in a frying pan, add the dashi and bring to the boil. Adjust the seasoning, adding chili garlic sauce, soy sauce, saké, black pepper, and garlic in that order. Finally, thicken with the kuzu.

5   Quickly mix the halibut cheeks and cooked bamboo shoots into the sauce. Pile on to plates and serve with the thinly sliced scallion (spring onion) and snowpeas (mangetouts).

アジのソテーと
スパイシーレモンドレッシング

Sautéed Horse Mackerel with Spicy Lemon Dressing

Here the fish's crisp skin sets off the succulent flesh and the fresh flavors are enhanced by the spicy lemon dressing.

serves 2
1 horse mackerel
sea salt
black pepper
flour
olive oil
vegetable oil for deep-frying
⅕ kamo eggplant (aubergine)
ginger strips
scallion (spring onion) whites, thinly sliced lengthways
finely chopped chives
Spicy Lemon Dressing (see page 246)

1   Fillet the fish lengthways, carefully cutting away the soft bones from the stomach area, picking out the bones from the darker flesh with fish tweezers and reserving the backbone. Score the flesh in a couple of places on each fillet with a sharp knife.

2   Season the fillets with salt and pepper, then coat well with flour. Heat the olive oil in a frying pan over a medium heat and sauté the fillets, skin side down, until the skin is nice and crisp. Then turn over and briefly sauté the flesh side.

3   Heat vegetable oil for deep-frying to a temperature of 340°F (170°C). Slice the eggplant (aubergine) into wheels and deep-fry these in the hot oil until browned and cooked through. Drain well on paper towel. Heat the vegetable oil for deep-frying this time to a temperature of 355°F (180°C) and fry the backbone of the fish until it is crunchy (bone senbei). Drain well on paper towel.

4   Place the fried eggplant on a serving plate. Lay the fried backbone and the sautéed fillets on top. Pile the ginger spears, onions, and finely chopped chives on top of those. Finally pour over some of the Spicy Lemon Dressing.

NOBU'S NOTES
•   When using larger, thicker jack mackerel, I would suggest cutting the fillets from the upper half of the fish in two.
•   If, when you fry the mackerel backbone, you hold the tail and head ends with chopsticks, it will turn back on itself when fried to create a decorative shape. Fry it like that until it is good and crisp.

タラバ蟹のクリーミースパイシーソース焼き
King Crab with Creamy Spicy Sauce

In this bold treatment for meaty king crab a slight lack of
delicate sweetness in the king crab meat is supplemented by the
Creamy Spicy Sauce.

serves 2
2 king crab legs
2 tablespoons crab roe
finely chopped scallions (spring onions)
4 tablespoons Creamy Spicy Sauce (see page 242)
chopped chives

1   Cook all but the thinnest (meatless) parts of the king crab
claws in boiling salted water until cooked through. Drain and,
when cool enough to handle, remove the cooked meat from the
shell, place on a toban (hotplate) and set on the heat.
2   Once the crab leg meat is hot, add the crab roe, the finely
chopped scallions (spring onions), and the Creamy Spicy Sauce.
Cook on the toban until lightly browned.
3   Finally, garnish with chopped chives.

NOBU'S NOTE
•   The Creamy Spicy Sauce should be made in small quantities
    and used as quickly as possible.

マッシュルームの陶板焼き
Mushroom Toban Yaki

This is a dish that enhances the flavors and textures of an
assortment of mushrooms with buttery aromas.

serves 2
2 shiitake mushrooms
1⅛ ounces (35g) eringi mushrooms
1 ounce (30g) shimeji mushrooms
1⅛ ounces (35g) enoki mushrooms
1 ounce (30g) maitake mushrooms
1 ounce (30g) beefsteak mushrooms
2 white mushrooms
1 ounce (30g) oyster mushrooms
grapeseed oil
2 tablespoons clarified butter
2 tablespoons saké
1 tablespoon light soy sauce
1 tablespoon freshly squeezed yuzu juice

1   Remove the base part of the shiitake mushroom stems. Cut
decorative slashes across the tops of the mushroom caps. Next,
cut all the mushrooms into bite-size pieces and split the clumps
of smaller mushrooms.
2   Flash-broil (grill) all of the mushrooms.dry under a very hot
broiler (grill).
3   Heat a toban (hotplate) thoroughly over a high heat. Pour
some grapeseed oil into the toban, add the clarified butter,
followed by the mushrooms. Immediately mix in the saké, soy
sauce, and the yuzu juice, and turn off the heat.
4   Serve covered with the toban lid, removing only when you
are ready to eat.

NOBU'S NOTES
•   Carefully select seven or eight different types of mushroom
    for their fragrance, flavor, and taste.
•   The trick here is to work quickly so that the mushrooms do
    not overcook. Serve the dish promptly to savor fully the
    enticing aromas.

タラバ蟹のクリーミースパイシーソース焼き
King Crab with Creamy Spicy Sauce

マッシュルームの陶板焼き
Mushroom Toban Yaki

キングクラブ　淡雪仕立て　トリュフがけ
King Crab White Soufflé with Truffle

grill

神戸牛のフィレ　アンティクーチョソース
Kobe Beef with Anti-cucho Sauce

Kobe fillet steak is complemented by two types of Peruvian togarashi sauce to create a truly innovative taste sensation.

serves 2
2 sweet potatoes
sea salt
5 fava (broad) beans
1 leek, quartered and very finely shredded lengthways
3½ ounces (100g) Kobe beef fillet
black pepper
Red Anti-cucho Sauce (see page 242)
Orange Anti-cucho Sauce (see page 242)

1　First prepare the accompanying vegetables: slice the sweet potato into rough ⅜ inch (1cm) rounds, bevel the edges, and cook in boiling salted water until just tender, then drain. Cook the fava (broad) beans in the same way, shell, and set aside. Deep-fry the leeks in hot oil until crisp and lightly colored.
2　Preheat the oven to 400°F (200°C, gas 6) and a dry frying pan. Season the beef with salt and pepper, brown it on all sides in the pan, then place in the preheated oven for 6 minutes, turning it over halfway through. Remove from the oven, wrap the cooked beef in foil and set aside to rest for 5 minutes.
3　Heat the red and orange Anti-cucho Sauces through in two separate small pans.
4　Place the cooked steak on plates and top with the sautéed leeks. Add the sweet potato and fava (broad) beans. Pour over the red and orange Anti-cucho Sauces.

NOBU'S NOTES
• Cook the steak medium-rare and select seasonal vegetables of your choice.
• When using the grill pan, press down on the meat to sear and rotate through 90° when you turn it over to get the desired lattice pattern on the surface. If you do not have a grill pan, sear a lattice shape on the surface using a red-hot metal skewer.
• Anti-cucho is a well-known Peruvian dish in which beef heart is skewered and grilled. We use the various anti-cucho sauces sourced from Peru in our cooking at Nobu.

伊勢海老のグリル　スパイシーレモンガーリックソース
Ise Lobster with Spicy Lemon Garlic Sauce

ラムチョップ　味噌アンティクーチョソース
Lamb Chop with Miso Anti-cucho Sauce

This is a Japanese take on lamb chops, accompanied by a Miso Anti-cucho Sauce.

serves 2
dried gourd shavings
sea salt
2 lamb chops
olive oil
black pepper
1 leek
5 fava (broad) beans

MISO ANTI-CUCHO SAUCE
1 tablespoon Nobu-style Saikyo Miso (see page 245)
1 tablespoon red Anti-cucho Sauce (see page 242)
1 tablespoon orange Anti-cucho Sauce (see page 242)

1　Rub some salt into the dried gourd shavings, rinse off with cold water, and then plunge into boiling water for about 2 minutes. Drain well.

2　Trim off any excess fat from the chops, pat clean with a paper towel, and shape neatly. Season and wrap the exposed chop bones carefully with the boiled gourd shavings.

3　Preheat the oven to 400°F (200°C, gas 6). Heat some olive oil in an ovenproof frying pan and quickly brown the lamb chops over a high heat, then transfer to the oven for about 4 minutes.

4　Make the Miso Anti-cucho Sauce: put all the ingredients into a small pan and blend together while heating.

5　Cut the leek into 1 inch (2cm) lengths and sauté lightly in a little more oil, then sear the surface of the leeks on the ridges of a grill pan.

6　At the same time, cook the fava (broad) beans in boiling salted water until they are just tender. Drain.

7　Pile the leeks on plates, pour over the sauce, scatter the beans around the plate to give a dynamic feel to the dish, then stand the chops on the leeks.

NOBU'S NOTE

• Using the gourd shavings gives the dish more of a Japanese feel than if you use foil, as well as helping to keep your guest's fingers clean!

鮎の笹焼き　青タデ・紅タデソース
Bamboo Roasted Ayu with Green and Red Tade Sauces

サーモングリルとベイビースピナッチ
Grilled Salmon with Baby Spinach Chips

鮎の笹焼き　青タデ・紅タデソース
Bamboo Roasted Ayu with Green and Red Tade Sauces

Wrapping in a bamboo leaf infuses the salted and griddled fish with a bamboo fragrance, given depth and complexity by the addition of the tade sauces.

serves 1

1 ayu

salt

3 bamboo leaves

1/3 ounce (10g) ayu tade

GREEN AND RED TADE SAUCES

1 ounce (30g) green tade

1 ounce (30g) red tade

3 tablespoons and 1 teaspoon rice vinegar

1 teaspoon sea salt

black pepper

3 tablespoons plus 1 teaspoon grapeseed oil

1   Preheat a griddle. Remove the slime from the ayu skin by rubbing with salt. Pat the fish dry with a paper towel, then sprinkle salt around the gills, fins, and tail. Sprinkle more salt lightly across the whole fish and cook on the griddle for 7 minutes. Keep the griddle hot.

2   Spread out a large sheet of foil. Spread a wet bamboo leaf on the foil and then place the ayu on the bamboo leaf. Put the ayu tade on top of the ayu and place another wet bamboo leaf on top of the ayu tade, then wrap the whole thing in the foil. Cook the package for 5 minutes on the griddle.

3   To make the Green and Red Tade Sauces: place the green and the red tade in separate containers, then blend each with half the rice vinegar, sea salt, pepper to taste, and grapeseed oil to make two different sauces.

4   Spread a fresh bamboo leaf on a plate. Unwrap the foil package and place the cooked ayu along the middle of the bamboo leaf, then pour over the two sauces.

NOBU'S NOTE

•   Pouring the red and green tade so that they do not mix will make the dish more colorful.

サーモングリルとベイビースピナッチ
Grilled Salmon with Baby Spinach Chips

A simple dressing of clarified butter and ponzu draws out the full taste of the lightly cooked salmon.

serves 2

vegetable oil for deep-frying

grapeseed oil

7 ounces (200g) boneless skinless salmon fillet

sea salt

black pepper

large handful baby spinach leaves, stalks removed

2 tablespoons clarified butter

1 tablespoon ponzu (see page 63)

3 tablespoons salmon roe

white part of scallions (spring onions), very thinly sliced
   lengthways

1   Heat vegetable oil for deep-frying to a temperature of 320°F (160°C).

2   Preheat a griddle. At the same time, heat some grapeseed oil in a frying pan and sear the seasoned salmon so that the outsides are browned. Place on the griddle and continue to cook to medium-rare.

3   Meanwhile pat the baby spinach leaves dry and deep-fry in the hot oil briefly until crisp. Drain well on paper towel.

4   Place the cooked salmon on plates. Pile the fried baby spinach on top of the salmon. Drizzle the clarified butter and ponzu over the spinach and salmon, sprinkle with salmon roe, and finally top with the scallion (spring onion) strips.

小ヤリイカのグリル
Grilled Koyari Squid

Easy-eating Koyari squid marinated in flavored extra virgin olive oil goes very well with a glass of wine.

serves 2
3 Koyari squid
1 zucchini (courgette)
a few chives

MARINADE
½ teaspoon sea salt
3 tablespoons extra virgin olive oil
1 teaspoon garlic (finely grated)
a little black pepper
a little soy sauce
1 tablespoon freshly squeezed yuzu juice

1　Remove the eyes, beaks, and entrails from the squid. Cut the zucchini (courgette) in half lengthways, then cut both halves into about 4 pieces of equal size. They should each end up just under 2 inches (4cm) long.

2　Place the squid and zucchini (courgette) in a bowl, add the marinade ingredients and mix well. Leave to marinate for about 20 minutes.

3　Preheat a grill pan and quickly cook the drained squid and the zucchini (courgette) until just cooked through. When the squid is ready, cut it into bite-size pieces.

4　Pile squid and courgette on to plates and scatter with chopped chives.

NOBU'S NOTE
• Soft Koyari squid should be used with the skin left on. If you overcook the squid, it will become tough and dry out, so be sure to cook quickly to retain its natural tenderness.

ブラックコッドの黒胡椒焼き
Black Pepper Crusted Black Cod

Fillets of black cod are cooked here with plenty of coarsely milled black pepper so that the aroma and flavor of the black pepper sing out.

serves 2
2 artichokes
8½ ounces (240g) black cod fillets
sea salt
black pepper
3 tablespoons olive oil
Teriyaki Balsamico Sauce (see page 243)
1 pickled ginger stem
white part of scallions (spring onions), very thinly sliced lengthways

1　Steam the artichokes for about 30 minutes. Peel away the leaves down to the heart. Cut away the top parts and discard, and use only the bottom part or heart.

2　Preheat the oven to 400°F (200°C, gas 6). Sprinkle the black cod fillets with some sea salt and cover well with lots of black pepper.

3　Put the olive oil into an ovenproof frying pan and set over a high heat. Fry the fish, skin side down, until it is crisp. Transfer to the preheated oven and bake for about 10 minutes.

4　Bring the Teriyaki Balsamico Sauce to a boil in a small pan, and continue to boil to reduce it until the sauce has a slightly thick consistency.

5　Place the fried black cod on plates and pile the finely shredded white scallions (spring onions) on top. Add the artichoke hearts and pickled ginger. Serve the Teriyaki Balsamico Sauce on the side.

NOBU'S NOTE
• Plenty of fragrant, coarsely ground black pepper should be sprinkled over the fish, particularly on the skin side. The trick here is to add considerably more than you think is enough!

小ヤリイカのグリル
Grilled Koyari Squid

ブラックコッドの黒胡椒焼き
Black Pepper Crusted Black Cod

トロのはがしのサッと焼き
Broiled Toro Back

地鶏のグリル　ワサビペッパーソース
Grilled Chicken with Wasabi Pepper Sauce

トロのはがしのサッと焼き

Broiled Toro Back

By lightly charring the toro back, the fatty part of the tuna belly which is normally quite firm when raw, the taste and texture are totally transformed into something seriously delicious.

serves 1
1 shiitake mushroom
a little butter
⅛ red onion, finely chopped
1¾ ounces (50g) toro (tuna belly)
sea salt
black pepper
a few chives, finely chopped
1 teaspoon aged balsamic vinegar

1   Slice the shiitake mushroom into pieces about ¹⁄₁₆ inch (2mm) thick. Heat some butter in a frying pan and sauté the slices lightly.
2   Using tweezers, peel away the meaty tendon strips from the back of the tuna with the meat that stays attached to them. Season with salt and pepper.
3   Put a wire rack over an open flame or barbecue coals or under the broiler (grill) and briefly sear the tendons for about 10-15 seconds, until crisp and cooked through.
4   Place the cooked toro on a plate. Combine the sautéed shiitake and finely chopped red onion, and pile on top of the fish. Add finely chopped chives. Spoon over the balsamic vinegar and serve.

NOBU'S NOTE
*   When seared, toro tendons acquire a melt-in-the-mouth texture, and become lovely and sweet.

トロのはがしのサッと焼き

地鶏のグリル　ワサビペッパーソース
Grilled Chicken with Wasabi Pepper Sauce

The texture of char-grilled chicken with crunchy skin gives us a taste of the earth's abundance, and invigorating wasabi stimulates the palate.

serves 2

1 boneless Anami black chicken breast, about 4½ ounces (130g)
1 boneless Anami black chicken thigh, about 7 ounces (200g)
sea salt
black pepper
3 green asparagus tips
1 teaspoon clarified butter
½ teaspoon finely grated garlic
3 tablespoons plus 1 teaspoon Wasabi Pepper Sauce (see page 244)
fresh wasabi, finely shredded

1　Preheat a grill pan and a griddle. Season the chicken breast and thigh with salt and pepper, and brown in the grill pan. Then heat on a griddle until cooked through, about 12 minutes.
2　At the same time, cook the asparagus in boiling salted water until tender. Drain well.
3　Heat the clarified butter and grated garlic in a frying pan. When you smell the garlic aroma, add the Wasabi Pepper Sauce, then more black pepper to taste. Immediately turn off the heat when the mixture comes to a boil.
4　Cut the broiled chicken into bite-size pieces. Place the thigh meat on plates and the breast meat on top of the thigh meat. Pile finely shredded fresh wasabi on the top. Pour over the Wasabi Pepper Sauce mix, and finally add the cooked asparagus.

NOBU'S NOTES

- Do not overboil the Wasabi Pepper Sauce. If you overheat it, the pepperiness and aromatic qualities of the wasabi will disappear.
- Cook the chicken just until the skin is crisp, but the flesh is still plump and moist.

マコモタケのクリーミースパイシーソース
Makomo-Dake with Creamy Spicy Sauce

The power of the raw ingredients in this dish are complemented by a piquant sauce and the fragrance of yuzu miso.

serves 2

1 ounce (30g) shelled raw shrimp (prawns)
1 ounce (30g) shelled scallops
vegetable oil for deep-frying
1 makomo-dake (water bamboo stalk)
2 tablespoons Creamy Spicy Sauce (see page 242)
1 teaspoon Yuzu Miso Sauce (see page 41)
braised lotus root
1 yama momo (small mountain peach)

1　Finely chop the shrimp (prawns) and scallops, and mix together.
2　Heat vegetable oil for deep-frying to a temperature of 340°F (170°C). Peel the makomo-dake and deep-fry for about 1 minute in the hot oil.
3　Preheat a broiler (grill). Cut the fried makomo-dake in half lengthways. Cover the rounded back part of the stalks with the minced shrimp and scallop. Shape the mince mixture as you spoon it onto the makomo-dake, then broil (grill) for about 2 minutes.
4　Spoon the Creamy Spicy Sauce and Yuzu Miso Sauce over the seafood mix and broil (grill) again until very lightly browned.
5　Serve on plates, together with the braised lotus root and the palate-cleansing yama momo.

マコモタケのクリーミースパイシーソース
Makomo-Dake with Creamy Spice Sauce

sus
h
i

NOBU Style 寿司とロールの盛り合わせ
Nobu-style Assorted Sushi & Rolls

Although based on classic techniques and basic ingredients, in many ways – choice of topping, combinations, construction, and technique – these represent a totally new way with sushi.

Simple Sushi

With one finger, press about a tablespoonful of Vinegared Sushi Rice (see page 190) into a firm oval in the palm of your hand. Spread with wasabi and place the chosen topping (see below) over that to cover the rice fairly neatly.

SUGGESTED TOPPINGS

For Seared Toro Sushi: Lightly sear the surface of 2 slices of toro (tuna belly), about ⅛ inch (3mm) thick. Allow to cool and then arrange on the vinegared rice.

For Young Yellowtail Sushi: Arrange 2 slices of young yellowtail fillet, about ⅛ inch (3mm) thick, on the vinegared rice and top with 2 thin slices of jalapeño, and a little finely grated garlic.

For Sea Bream Sushi: Arrange 2 slices of sea bream fillet, about ⅛ inch (3mm) thick, on the vinegared rice and top with 2 coriander leaves, a small quantity of rocoto chili paste, a little flaked salt, and a small drizzle of Yuzu Lemon Sauce (see page 82).

For Halibut Sushi: Arrange 2 slices of halibut fillet, about ⅛ inch (3mm) thick, on the vinegared rice and top with ½ green shiso leaf, a little flaked salt, and a small quantity of freshly squeezed lemon juice.

For New-Style Salmon Sushi: Arrange 2 slices of salmon fillet, about ⅛ inch (3mm) thick, on the vinegared rice and drizzle over some New-Style Oil (see page 82). Top with some chive stalks and ginger spears.

Sushi Rolls

As well as Vinegared Sushi Rice (see page 190), to make sushi rolls you'll usually need sheets of toasted nori and/or sheets of fresh daikon (cut from it using the katsuramuki technique). I often use the two in combination, with the daikon forming the outer layer of a roll's wrapping and the nori an inner layer. Of course, sometimes sushi rolls don't have any such solid outer layers, only a thick coating of toasted sesame seeds (see Shrimp Tempura Roll, below).

1   Place the daikon peel and/or nori sheets (cut to the same size) stretching away from you. Make sure you place the nori dull side facing upwards. Spread the vinegared rice out evenly over the nori. Using one hand to prevent rice spilling over the ends of the nori, gently press down the rice with the fingertips of your other hand. Leave about 2 inches (5cm) free on the far side, and ⅜ inch (1cm) free on the side nearest you.

2   Apply a streak of wasabi down the middle of the bed of vinegared rice, and then a line of the chosen filling(s) as set out below.

3   Firmly roll up from the end nearest you, taking care not to squeeze out the contents.

4   Cut the roll into pieces and arrange on a plate. Serve some pickled ginger on the side.

SUGGESTED FILLINGS

For Spicy Tuna Roll: 1 ounce (30g) red meat tuna fillet cut into long strips, topped with a little smear of Creamy Spice Sauce (see page 242) and some chive stalks.

For Vegetable Roll: First sprinkle the rice with toasted white sesame seeds , then arrange on it some strips of avocado flesh, some small okra fingers, some yamagobo, cooked green asparagus spears, one or two green shiso leaves, chives and a little kaiware daikon.

For Shrimp Tempura Roll: Instead of arranging the rice on sheets of daikon and/or nori, place it on a sheet of plastic wrap. Sprinkle toasted white sesame seeds over the rice and then use the plastic wrap to turn the whole thing over. At that stage, place a sheet of nori on the rice. Arrange some Shrimp Tempura (see page 108) and cooked green asparagus spears in a line along the nori. Squeeze some Creamy Spice Sauce (see page 242) in a line alongside the shrimp and roll up.

酢飯／シャリ
Vinegared Sushi Rice

This is the single most important element in the whole sushi experience. Cook the rice so it is nice and plump, then quickly spread it around using a rice paddle with a slicing motion so that the grains maintain their glossiness.

makes 5 cups

25½ ounces (720g) short-grain rice

SUSHI RICE VINEGAR

7 fluid ounces (200ml) Japanese red vinegar

2 tablespoons plus 2 teaspoons sea salt

1 tablespoon mirin

9 tablespoons plus 2 teaspoons granulated sugar

1½-inch (4cm) square sheet of konbu

1   To make the sushi rice vinegar: bring 5¼ fluid ounces (150ml) of the red vinegar to a simmer in a small pan over a medium heat with the salt, mirin and sugar until the sugar dissolves (do not let it boil). Add the konbu and take off the heat. When cool, add the remaining vinegar (this is done because the heating tends to destroy the bouquet of the vinegar). This will give enough sushi rice vinegar to make two batches of sushi rice of the size given here.

2   Thoroughly wash the rice (see note below), then soak it in cold water for about 30 minutes in the winter and 15 minutes in the summer (although the exact time will depend on how hard the rice is. Drain in a sieve.

3   Transfer to a bowl and add 31½ fluid ounces (900ml) fresh cold water to the rice. Bring to a boil over high heat, and boil for 1 minute, then reduce the heat to low and cook for 5 minutes more. Finally increase the heat to high again for 10 seconds only. Take off the heat. For vinegared rice, the rice needs to be cooked so that the grains stay quite firm. Allow the cooked rice to sit for about 15 minutes, then drain off any excess water.

4   While the rice is still hot, wipe the inside of a rice tub or similar wide shallow container well with a piece of konbu steeped in vinegared water. Spread the rice out thinly. Slicing the rice with a rice paddle or flat wooden spoon, sprinkle half the prepared vinegar evenly over the rice. Cut through the rice from the bottom up so that it is well turned over. Continue to blend in the vinegar, slicing diagonally and moving the rice to one side of the tub. Cover with a well-wrung-out damp cloth until ready to use, but do use the rice before it becomes too hard.

NOBU'S NOTES

*   Wash the rice in a big bowl filled with cold water. Change the water frequently as you begin to wash the rice. This will get rid of excess starch. When the water stops being cloudy and is clear, the washing is complete.
*   When slicing with the rice paddle, the action should be swift and rhythmical. Be careful not to over-stir as this will make the rice sticky.

魚介類の贅沢バラ寿司
Seafood Bara Sushi

This triumphant culmination of the art takes sushi-making to new heights in a bold expression of the seasons.

serves 10

10 shrimps (prawns)
3 king crab legs
10 mantis shrimp
10 Japanese shad
rice vinegar
piece of konbu
1 boneless skinless sea bass fillet
5 small boneless skinless porgy fillets
4 boneless skinless sea eel fillets
1 abalone in the shell
5 tokobushi abalone
5 red clams
5 scallops
3½ ounces (100g) small scallops
5 Ishigaki (giant) clams
5 razor shell clams
5 cockles
7 ounces (200g) dried gourd shavings
7 ounces (200g) shiitake mushrooms
Vinegared Sushi Rice (see opposite)
5 eggs
3½ ounces (100g) young ginger
cooked green peas
shiitake mushrooms
kinome (sansho sprigs)
bofu (siler) sprigs

1   Prepare the sushi topping ingredients in advance. Plunge the shrimp (prawns), king crab legs, and mantis shrimp briefly into boiling water. Remove the shells. Fry the shrimp tails, and set aside.

2   Marinate the whole shad in vinegar with the konbu for 2 hours. Plunge the drained shad, sea bass and porgy into boiling water, remove and immediately plunge into ice-cold water. Broil (grill) the seasoned eel fillets until cooked through. Shell all the other shellfish and briefly broil (grill) all the shellfish meat until just cooked. Cut all the fish and shellfish into bite-size pieces. Boil the dried gourd shavings and shiitake until tender and chop into conveniently sized chunks.

3   Make the vinegared rice (see opposite). Beat the eggs lightly and pour into a large lightly oiled frying pan over a high heat. Cook, stirring, until it forms a light just-set omelet. Roll up, tip on to a plate and cut across into shreds. Very finely shred the ginger.

4   In a large wooden rice tub or large plate, pile up the vinegared rice, with the dried gourd shavings and shiitake mixed through it in soft drifts. Scatter the above prepared toppings over the rice in a colorful arrangement. Finally, scatter the green peas, the kinome (lightly pulverized to extract the aroma), and the bofu sprigs in an attractive manner over the toppings.

NOBU'S NOTES

- This is not raw sushi, so all the fresh ingredients need to be prepared in advance.
- This is a really magnificent dish if you go overboard in finding the finest seasonal materials. Any combination of shellfish, vegetables, and meat is possible for Bara Sushi. This is just one illustration of the sort of menu that can be created.

魚介類の贅沢バラ寿司
Seafood Bara Sushi

ソフトシェルクラブロール
Soft Shell Crab Roll

サーモンスキンロール
Salmon Skin Roll

ソフトシェルクラブロール
Soft Shell Crab Roll

This Nobu sushi signature dish is one form of sushi roll that truly embodies the borderless nature of taste.

for 1 roll
vegetable oil for deep-frying
1 largish soft shell crab
potato flour
1 sheet daikon (katsuramuki cut)
1 sheet toasted nori (cut in half)
4½ ounces (130g) Vinegared Sushi Rice (see page 190)
wasabi
1 teaspoon asatsuki chives
1 teaspoon flying fish roe
⅛ stoned peeled avocado
pickled ginger

1   Heat vegetable oil for deep-frying to a temperature of 355°F (180°C). Dust the soft shell crab lightly with the potato flour and deep-fry in the hot oil until crisp. Drain well on paper towel.
2   Place the daikon peel on a chopping board, stretching away from you, and cut to the same width as the nori. Place the nori, dull side facing upwards, squarely on the daikon peel. Spread the vinegared rice out evenly over the nori. Using one hand to prevent rice spilling over the ends of the nori, gently press down the rice with the fingertips of your other hand. Leave about 2 inches (5cm) free on the far side, and ⅜ inch (1cm) free on the side nearest you.
3   Apply a streak of wasabi down the middle of the bed of vinegared rice, and then a line of finely chopped chives and the flying fish roe.
4   Cut the fried soft shell crab in half, and add it to the roll, along with the avocado cut into long segments. Firmly roll up from the end nearest you, taking care not to squeeze out the contents.
5   Cut the roll into 6 and arrange the pieces on a plate. Put some pickled ginger on the side.

NOBU'S NOTE
•   When spreading the vinegared rice over the nori, do not squash it too firmly.

サーモンスキンロール
Salmon Skin Roll

This sushi roll uses smoked salmon skin grilled to a fragrant crispness and is laced with luscious avocado.

for 1 roll
1½ ounces (40g) smoked salmon skin
1 sheet daikon (katsuramaki peel cut)
1 sheet toasted nori, cut in half
4½ ounces (130g) Vinegared Sushi Rice (see page 190)
wasabi
1 teaspoon toasted white sesame seeds
2 green shiso leaves, halved
1 teaspoon chopped asatsuki chives
⅛ stoned peeled avocado, cut into long segments
1 yamagobo root
½ tablespoon kaiware daikon
small quantity of finely shredded dried bonito flakes
pickled ginger

1   Grill the smoked salmon skin until crisp over an open flame or hot coals. Cut it into ⅛-inch (3mm) strips.
2   Place the daikon peel on a chopping board, stretching away from you and cut to the same width as the nori. Place the nori, dull side facing upwards, squarely on the daikon peel. Spread the vinegared rice evenly over the nori. Using one hand to prevent rice spilling over the ends of the nori, gently press down the rice with the fingertips of your other hand. Leave about 2 inches (5cm) free on the far side, and ⅜ inch (1cm) free on the side nearest you. Try not to squash the vinegared rice too firmly.
3   Apply a streak of wasabi down the middle of the bed of vinegared rice, then arrange the sesame seeds, the shiso leaves, the chopped chives, the avocado, the yamagobo (cut into the same length as the width of the nori), the kaiware daikon, the grilled salmon skin strips, and the shredded bonito flakes. Firmly roll up, taking care not to squeeze out the contents.
4   Cut each roll into 6 equal pieces (shown divided into 3 in the photograph). Serve with some pickled ginger on the side.

NOBU'S NOTE
•   When cutting the sushi roll, slightly dampen a very sharp knife, and slice carefully and firmly.

魚ソーメン　ポモドーロソース

White Fish Somen with Pomodoro Sauce

However unusual they sound, the fish somen made here are not all that far removed from Italian "pasta fresca" and so marry well with my version of a classic Italian sauce.

serves 2

fish somen
18 ounces (500g) white fish surimi
2 egg whites
2 tablespoons dashi (see page 97)
2 tablespoons katakuriko
small quantity of sea salt

POMODORO SAUCE
10½ ounces (300g) fruit tomatoes
3 tablespoons and 1 teaspoon olive oil
2 tablespoons coarsely chopped onion
sea salt
a little black pepper
2 basil leaves

1　Make the fish somen: put the surimi, egg whites, dashi, katakuriko, and sea salt in a food processor, and process until well mixed and of a thick consistency.

2　Prepare a suitable polythene food bag. Open a hole by cutting one of the bottom corners off with a pair of scissors. Spoon the paste into the bag.

3　Boil some water in a pan, then turn down the heat to low. Keeping the water at a medium heat (about 175-195°F/80°-90°C), squeeze lengths of the paste out of the bag into the boiling water. Heat gently for about 3-4 minutes. As the somen float to the top, scoop them out with a small strainer and plunge them immediately into ice-cold water to chill and stop them cooking.

4　Make the Pomodoro Sauce: peel off the fruit tomato skins by first immersing them in hot water, then lightly simmer briefly until the skins come off readily.

5　Heat the olive oil in a pan and fry the onion. Once the onions start to color, add the skinned fruit tomatoes, crushing them at the same time. Turn the heat up high for a moment and, as soon as the sauce boils, reduce the heat to medium, and simmer for about 15 minutes. Adjust the taste with the salt and pepper, add the basil, then turn off the heat. Chill.

6　Dress the fish somen with the chilled Pomodoro Sauce on a plate and garnish with basil.

NOBU'S NOTE

• When putting the white fish paste into the hot water, squeeze it out in a single steady stream. Do not allow the water to boil at any time.

魚ソーメン　ポモドーロソース

ハラペーニョ切りそば

Jalapeño Soba

As a change from normal soba, those in this gem of a dish are made with jalapeño to deliver a fiery kick after the refreshing sweetness of the broth.

serves 2

7 ounces (200g) soba (buckwheat) flour

1¾ ounces (50g) strong plain flour

⅓ ounce (10g) jalapeño chili, deseeded and finely chopped, plus more slices for garnish

CLEAR SOBA BROTH

7 fluid ounces (200ml) dashi (see page 97)

3 tablespoons soy sauce

4 teaspoons mirin

⅔ ounce (20g) granulated sugar

⅔ ounce (20g) dried bonito flakes

TO SERVE

yakumi (grated fresh wasabi)

sliced and chopped jalapeño

finely chopped scallion (spring onion)

1   First make the soba broth: put the dashi into a pan and heat over a high heat. Add the soy sauce, mirin, and sugar. Lastly add the bonito flakes, then turn off the heat. When the bonito flakes have sunk to the bottom, strain and allow the liquid to cool.

2   Make the jalapeño soba: sprinkle the soba flour and strong flour into a bowl, and mix well.

3   Put chopped jalapeño in a blender with 4 fluid ounces (120ml) water. Liquidize to make "jalapeño water".

4 Combine half this "jalapeño water" with the mixed flours in the bowl, blending with a rhythmical action. Begin by rubbing the dough between your fingertips, gradually using bigger and bigger hand movements to mix. When the mixture resembles bread dough, add the rest of the jalapeño water and mix until the dough is soft but firm.

5 Bring the dough together, making sure that the moisture is evenly distributed. Knead the dough firmly, pressing down on it with the lower hand/wrist area. Sprinkle some flour over the kneading surface. Form the dough into a ball and lightly flour. Flatten out (stretch) the dough, pressing down with the palms of your hands. Continuing to sprinkle flour on the dough, use a rolling pin to flatten the dough to about ¹⁄₃₂ inch (1mm) thickness evenly all over.

6   Fold the sheet of dough over like a belt about 8 inches (20cm) wide and place on a floured chopping board. Place a komaita (wooden chopping board used to cut noodles) on a solid surface. Then, sliding the board along, cut the dough with a soba bocho. Handle the cut soba noodles lightly as you smooth out and arrange the strands.

7   Bring a large pan of water to a boil, place the cut noodles in the water and cook for about 30 seconds. Drain the noodles through a zaru (a bamboo colander), then plunge immediately into cold water. Drain lightly.

8   Pile the jalapeño soba on a zaru or into bowls. Garnish with a whole jalapeño or slices. Serve with the soba broth, yakumi, chopped jalapeño, and chopped scallions (spring onions).

NOBU'S NOTE

•   When making the jalapeño water in the juicer, if you leave a few flecks of the chili in the liquid instead of completely liquidizing it, these will add flavor and color. However, if the fragments are too big, the soba dough will not bind properly, and when you come to knead it, the dough will tend to break. Try to stop the juicing at just the right point if you can.

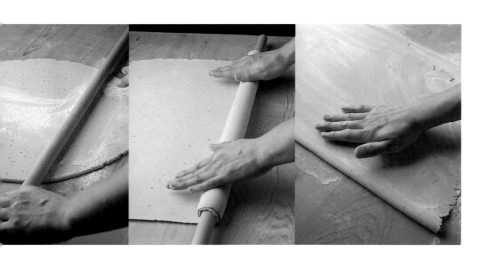

たで切りそば
Tade Soba

コリアンダー切りそば
Cilantro Soba

sert

des

バンブーゼリー
Bamboo Jello

バンブーゼリー
Bamboo Jello

Served in green bamboo cups, these delicately colored jellos and puddings make a feast for the eyes. Bamboo sections like these may be bought ready made – there are even porcelain dishes made to look like bamboo sections – but you could use any suitable tall container.

Mango Pudding

serves 4

6 ounces (180g) mango purée
1 ounce (30g) granulated sugar
5½ fluid ounces (160ml) evaporated milk
⅔ ounce (20g) coconut purée
¹⁄₁₆ ounce (2g) gelatin
2 tablespoons whipping cream,
  beaten to soft peaks
2 teaspoons lemon juice
1¼ teaspoons rum

1 Heat the mango purée and granulated sugar together gently in a pan, stirring, until the sugar dissolves and then allow to cool.

2 Put the evaporated milk and coconut purée in a pan and heat to just below boiling point. Remove from the heat.

3 When the temperature drops to below 140°F (60°C), add the gelatin and mix in. Allow to cool a little further, then mix in the blended mango purée and granulated sugar.

4 Fold the mixture once, then, in a cool place, blend in the whipped cream, lemon juice and finally the rum.

5 Pour into the bamboo cylinders, filling them about three-quarters full. Chill to set.

Tofu Pudding

serves 4

4½ fluid ounces (125ml) soy milk
3 fluid ounces (90ml) milk
1½ ounces (45g) granulated sugar
¹⁄₁₆ ounce (2g) gelatin
2 tablespoons fresh whipping cream
3 tablespoons and 1 teaspoon sour cream
1½ teaspoons Cointreau
½ teaspoon lemon juice
⅔ ounce (20g) fresh yuba

    LILY ROOT BOILED WITH LEMON
    5½ ounces (160g) lily root
    5¼ fluid ounces (150ml) mineral water
    3½ ounces (100g) granulated sugar
    peel and juice of 1 lemon
    3 tablespoons and 1 teaspoon honey

1 Make the lily root boiled with lemon. Soak the lily root in cold water, rinse it well, then carefully cut out the black part with a bocho.

2 Put the mineral water, sugar, lemon peel and juice, and the honey in a pan, and bring to a boil. Turn the heat down to low, add the lily root and simmer for about 15minutes. Using a bamboo skewer, check to see if the lily root is hot right through, then remove pan from the heat. Decant into a bowl, cover with plastic wrap, and store in the fridge.

3 Put the soy milk, milk, and half the granulated sugar in a pan, and heat to just below boiling point. Remove from the heat and, when its temperature drops to below 140°F (60°C), mix in the gelatin blended together with the remaining sugar.

4 As the mixture cools further and thickens, blend in the fresh and sour creams, then add the Cointreau and lemon juice.

5 Pour a little of the mixture into the bamboo cylinders and allow to harden. Add some slices of the lily root and its lemon liqor, and the fresh yuba. Add more of the creamy mixture on top. Chill to set.

NOBU'S NOTES

- This is a convenient quantity of lilly root to prepare at one time, but you will have some left over. It will keep well in the refrigerator and can be used with a wide range of desserts.

Cherry Jello

serves 4

4½ fluid ounces (125ml) Matsuhisa Chardonnay
4½ fluid ounces (125ml) mineral water
1¾ ounces (50g) granulated sugar
⅓ ounce (10g) gelatin
1⅓ teaspoons lemon juice
1 tablespoon and 1 teaspoon cherry brandy
1 teaspoon orange flower water
12 stoned cherries

1   Put the Chardonnay, mineral water, and half the granulated sugar in a pan. Bring to a boil so that the alcohol can evaporate off.
2   Remove from the heat. When its temperature drops to below 140°F (60°C), mix in the gelatin blended together with the remaining sugar.
3   Allow the mixture to cool further, then add the lemon juice and cherry brandy, and allow to cool until the mixture thickens. Finish by adding the orange flower water.
4   Pour half the mixture into the bamboo cylinders. Add 3 cherries to each, then pour in a little more of the mixture. Allow to harden so that the cherries do not float to the surface, then fill up to the rims with more of the mixture. Chill to set.

TO SERVE

1   Lay a bamboo leaf out on a Japanese serving dish. Line up the finished jellos and puddings on the leaf.
2   For the mango puddings, cut a peeled mango into cubes, and fill the bamboo cylinders to the brim with the chunks.
3   For the tofu puddings, peel a little yuzu skin and place in the center, then decorate with kinome (sansho sprigs).
4   For the cherry jelly, place a little silver leaf on top.

NOBU'S NOTES

*   Powdered gelatin is tasteless and odorless, so it is ideal for making jellos.
*   The melt-in-the-mouth texture is what makes the jello so wonderful. As the subtle balance is entirely dependent on the quantities, make sure you measure these out exactly.
*   If you use fresh bamboo cylinders, be sure to store them in the refrigerator.

バナナスプリングロール
Banana Egg Roll

Fruits in season are served here with mango sherbet and chocolate ice cream wrapped up in a piping-hot banana spring roll. Note that the chocolate ice cream needs to be started a day before everything else.

serves 4

2 green shiso leaves

4 egg (spring) roll wrappers

3 bananas, sliced

small quantity sweetened chocolate, grated

small quantity flour

vegetable oil, for deep-frying

small quantity sliced almonds

SAUTÉED BANANA

3 bananas

5¼ ounces (150g) granulated sugar

1 ounce (30g) unsalted butter

1 ounce (30g) fresh cream

1 tablespoon rum

ICING

1¾ ounces (50g) fine rice flour, plus more for dusting

4 fluid ounces (120ml) water

1¾ ounces (50g) granulated sugar

katakuriko

1   Make the sautéed bananas: cut the bananas into ⅝-inch (1.5cm) thick slices.

2   Put the sugar and a small quantity of water into a frying pan and heat until it forms caramel. Add the butter and, when blended with the caramel, add the fresh cream.

3   Before the caramel hardens, add the banana slices a few at a time, and sauté lightly. Using a fork, turn the slices and sauté on the other sides. Finally add the rum to enrich the aroma, and transfer to a metal tray to cool.

4   Make the icing: combine the rice flour, water, and granulated sugar, then strain.

5   Put the strained mixture into a pan over a medium heat. Using a wooden spatula, knead until it forms a ball. When you have finished kneading, place the ball on to a katakuriko or floured metal tray and allow to cool.

6   Make the banana egg (spring) rolls: place half a green shiso leaf just below the middle of each egg (spring) roll wrapper. Then arrange alternating fresh banana and sautéed banana slices along the middle. Cut the icing into thin strips and lay on top of the banana, then place a little sweetened chocolate on top of the icing. Roll up the egg (spring) roll. Make a paste from a little flour and water, and brush some of this all over the outside of the wrappers to seal them in place. Roll in the sliced almonds so that they stick.

7   Heat oil for deep-frying to a temperature of 355°F (180°C). Fry the egg (spring) rolls and in the hot oil until well colored. Drain well.

NOBU'S NOTE

•   When sautéing the bananas, do so very carefully over a low heat, so that they do not start to break up.

バナナスプリングロール
Banana Egg Roll

Mango Sherbet

18 ounces (500g) mango purée
10½ fluid ounces (300ml) mineral water
5¼ ounces (150g) granulated sugar
2 tablespoons lemon juice
1½ ounces (40g) liquid glucose
2 tablespoons and 2 teaspoons Amaretto
3½ fluid ounces (100ml) Matsuhisa Chardonnay

1 Put the mango purée, mineral water, sugar, and lemon juice in a pan, and heat to just below boiling point. Turn off the heat, add the liquid glucose, then strain.
2 Add the Amaretto and Chardonnay. Pour into an ice-cream maker and freeze.

NOBU'S NOTE
*   Purées of the Indian mango variety Alfonso are thicker and sweeter than most other purées, and are best for sherbets and puddings.

Chocolate Ice Cream

5¼ fluid ounces (150ml) milk
10½ fluid ounces (300ml) heavy (double) cream
⅓ vanilla bean (pod), split and the seeds scraped out
6 egg yolks
2½ ounces (75g) granulated sugar
8¾ ounces (250g) sweetened chocolate, chopped
2 tablespoons and 2 teaspoons Cointreau

1 Put the milk, cream, and vanilla bean (pod) and seeds in a pan, and bring to a boil.
2 Mix together the egg yolks and sugar in a bowl. Add the hot milk mixture, return the contents of the bowl to the pan and put back over a gentle heat, stirring, to make a custard. Fish out the pieces of vanilla pod (bean). Mix in the chopped chocolate and leave overnight.
3 The next day, stir in the Cointreau, pour into an ice-cream machine and freeze.

NOBU'S NOTE
*   Use chocolate with as a high a cocoa content as you can find (I used one with 71% content here).

Chocolate Macaroons

3¼ ounces (95g) ground almonds
⅓ ounce (10g) cocoa powder
2½ ounces (75g) confectioner's (icing) sugar
2⅔ ounces (80g) egg whites
3 ounces (85g) granulated sugar

1 Put the ground almonds, cocoa powder, and confectioner's (icing) sugar in a bowl. Swirl around a couple of times to mix.
2 Put the egg whites into the bowl of a mixer and process at a high speed, gradually adding the granulated sugar to form a meringue mixture.
3 When the meringue mixture forms soft peaks, add the almond mixture, stirring it in with a rubber spatula until glossy.
4 Put the mixture into a pastry bag. Squeeze the mixture through the metal nozzle on to silicone baking parchment, forming little round dome shapes. Leave for 1 hour.
5 Preheat the oven to 325°F (160°C, gas 3) and bake the macaroons for 10 minutes.

NOBU'S NOTE
*   I use cocoa powder to flavor the macaroons, but you could just as well use powdered green tea, etc., for a totally different taste.

Tropical Sauce

1 teaspoon orange flower water

SAUCE BASE:
1¾ ounces (50g) mango purée
1¾ ounces (50g) passion fruit purée
1 ounce (30g) banana purée
1 ounce (30g) coconut purée
2 tablespoons rum
1 ounce (30g) granulated sugar
3 tablespoons and 1 teaspoon mineral water

1 First make the sauce base by putting all its ingredients in a pan, placing it over the heat and bringing the mixture to a simmer. Sieve the mixture and allow to cool.
2 Finally, stir in the orange flower water.

Chocolate Sauce

4 tablespoons milk
3 tablespoons and 1 teaspoon fresh whipping cream
1¾ ounces (50g) sweetened chocolate, chopped

Bring the milk and fresh cream to the boil, then stir in the chopped chocolate until you have a smooth sauce.

TO SERVE

chocolate spirals
silver leaf
seasonal fruit (the photograph shows passion fruit, raspberries, cherries, and physalis fruit)
chervil sprigs

1 Spread the tropical and chocolate sauces on a plate. Place the fried egg (spring) roll on the sauces.
2 Arrange 2 macaroons on the plate, along with the mango sherbet and chocolate ice cream.
3 Decorate with chocolate spirals and sprinkle over silver leaf. Add fruits in season, and a chervil sprig lends a dash of green.

NOBU'S NOTE
• Serve the banana while it is still piping hot.

パッションフルーツパスタ

Passion Fruit Pasta

This combination of warm sauce, ice cream, and smooth jello pasta is incredibly popular in the restaurants.

Passion Fruit Pasta Jello

5¾ ounces (165g) passion fruit purée
5¾ fluid ounces (165ml) Matsuhisa Chardonnay
7 fluid ounces (200ml) mineral water
2½ green shiso leaves
6 ounces (180g) granulated sugar
1 ounce (30g) pearl agar

1   Put all the ingredients other than the pearl agar in a pan and bring to a boil.
2   Skim off any scum, add the pearl agar and blend in well. Pass the mixture through a sieve into a metal tray and chill in the fridge.
3   When the jello solidifies, cut it into long lengths to resemble pasta. Serve about 1¾ ounces (50g) per person.

Rock Salt Ice Cream

13½ fluid ounces (400ml) milk
10½ fluid ounces (300ml) fresh whipping cream
1 tablespoon and 1 teaspoon skimmed milk
14 ounces (400g) condensed milk
⅛ ounce (4g) rock salt (Fleur de Sel de Guérande)

1   Put the milk, fresh cream, and skimmed milk in a pan, and heat to just below boiling point. Then turn off the heat, add the condensed milk, and mix well. Sieve and chill.
2   Once the base is chilled, put it in an ice-cream maker and freeze. Add the rock salt just before the ice cream has finished churning. (If you add the rock salt at the beginning, it will dissolve.)

パッションフルーツパスタ
Passion Fruit Pasta

Grapefruit Sauté

1 grapefruit
2 tablespoons olive oil
½ green shiso leaf

1 Separate the grapefruit into peeled segments. Lightly heat the olive oil in a frying pan and sauté both sides of the grapefruit segments over a low heat. The fruit will break up more easily when sautéed, so be careful not to overheat or the grapefruit will collapse completely. Scatter with chopped shiso leaf when done.
2 Break up the fruit by pressing it with the back of a fork.
3 Place the grapefruit on to a metal tray and soak up all the moisture thoroughly with paper towel.
4 Chill.

Coconut Nage

2⅔ ounces (80g) egg whites
2 tablespoons Malibu liqueur
  NAGE BASE
  10½ fluid ounces (300ml) milk
  13½ fluid ounces (400ml) coconut milk
  ⅔ ounce (20g) coconut powder
  5¼ ounces (150g) granulated sugar

1 First make the nage base by putting all its ingredients in a pan and heating. Turn off the heat just before it reaches boiling point and allow to cool to room temperature.
2 When the temperature of the base falls to around 140°F (60°C), fold in the egg whites and liqueur. Keeping the temperature at about 140°F (60°C), whisk to a foam with a hand whisk.

NOBU'S NOTES
• Once it foams, keep the coconut nage temperature at about around 140°F (60°C).
• This is a convenient amount of nage base to make, but you will probably have some left over. It will keep for a day or two in the refrigerator and can be used with many desserts. You can flavor it variously with any liqueur or fruit syrup.

TO SERVE

chopped shiso and some whole leaves
grapeseed oil
olive oil
passion fruit
confectioner's (icing) sugar

1 Fry some shiso leaves in grapeseed oil. Drain them well on paper towels.
2 Using a 2-inch (6cm) diameter circular mold, pack the rock salt ice cream on to a chilled plate.
3 Put a full tablespoon of the sautéed grapefruit on top of the ice cream, and pile the pasta jello on top of the grapefruit.
4 Pour the foaming coconut nage around the mold, then remove the mold.
5 Dot some olive oil and chopped shiso around the rim of the plate, and stick one leaf into the rock salt ice cream. Scoop out the seeds from the passion fruit and put these on the top in the middle, and garnish with fried shiso leaves. Finally, use a tea strainer to sprinkle over the confectioner's (icing) sugar.

NOBU'S NOTE
• Enjoy the texture contrast of the chilled jello and the fleshiness of the passion fruit.

レイヤード　ヘーゼルナッツ　ケーキ
Layered Hazelnut Cake

レイヤード　ヘーゼルナッツ　ケーキ

Layered Hazelnut Cake

Layers of iced cake and berries provide more subtle sweetness for the grown-ups. Note that the Hazelnut Wafers and the Caramel Ice Cream need to be started at least a day ahead of serving.

Hazelnut Wafers

serves 20

21½ ounces (600g) shelled eggs
12½ ounces (350g) vanilla sugar
⅛ ounce (5g) ground cinnamon
8 ounces (225g) ground hazelnuts
2½ ounces (75g) cake crumbs
1½ ounces (40g) cornstarch (cornflour)
3½ ounces (100ml) hazelnut oil

1   Mix the eggs, vanilla sugar, and cinnamon in a bowl.

2   Mix (by hand) the hazelnut powder, cake crumbs, and cornstarch (cornflour) in a separate bowl, making sure the cornstarch is thoroughly blended in.

3   In a third bowl, combine the contents of the other two. Mix in the hazelnut oil (carefully to avoid creating bubbles). Leave overnight to rest.

4   Next day, preheat the oven to 340°F (170°C, gas 3½). Divide the rested mixture into 4 equal amounts and place each on a sheet of silicone baking parchment. Using a palette knife, form them into rectangles about 1⁄16 inch (2mm) thick.

5   Bake in the preheated oven for 15-20 minutes (if you bake for too long, the flavor will deteriorate, so try to avoid browning the wafers). When cool, store in the refrigerator.

Caramel Ice Cream

serves 20

19¾ ounces (565g) granulated sugar
54 fluid ounces (1.5 litres) fresh whipping cream, warmed
18 egg yolks
15¾ fluid ounces (450ml) milk
5 tablespoons Toschi Nocello (Italian walnut liqueur)

1   Put 1 pound (450g) of the granulated sugar into a pan. Heat until it forms a caramel. If the caramel becomes too thick, it will be too rich, so stop while it remains relatively light and turns a pale gold. Stir in the warmed fresh cream.

2   Mix the eggs yolks and remaining granulated sugar in a bowl. Stir in the caramel and cream mixture, then return to the pan and heat gently until it thickens to form a custard. Stir the milk into the custard, pass through a sieve, and leave overnight.

3   Add the liqueur to the rested custard, divide the mixture into 3 equal parts and process these in an ice cream maker until frozen.

NOBU'S NOTE

• Since this is a fresh ice cream, consume it all within 2 days at the very most.

Hazelnut Succès

serves 20
6 ounces (180g) ground hazelnuts
7 ounces (200g) confectioner's (icing) sugar
8½ ounces (240g) egg whites
2½ ounces (75g) granulated sugar
1¾ ounces (50g) Royaltines (crispy fried crêpes), finely crushed
small quantity of sweetened chocolate

1 Sieve together the ground hazelnut and confectioner's (icing) sugar twice.
2 Whisk the egg whites and the granulated sugar until they reach the soft peak stage, forming a meringue.
3 Add the ground hazelnut mixture and crushed Royaltines to the meringue, folding it in lightly so as not to crush the air bubbles.
4 Preheat the oven to 325°F (160°C, gas 3). Place the mixture in a pastry bag and squeeze through a large nozzle on to a metal tray in long thick lines. Bake dry in the oven, about 15 minutes and leave to cool.
5 Once cooled, cover with sweetened chocolate and slice into 2-inch (6cm) widths.

NOBU'S NOTE
• If you are going to keep the Hazelnut Succès after it is sliced, store in the freezer.

Roast Hazelnuts

serves 20
10½ ounces (300g) whole hazelnuts
5¼ ounces (150g) granulated sugar

1 Roast the whole hazelnuts in a dry frying pan until lightly browned.
2 Preheat the oven to 350°F (180°C, gas 5). Lightly crush the hazelnuts with a rolling pin, blend them with the granulated sugar and a little water. Bake dry in the oven, about 15 minutes.

NOBU'S NOTE
• I use large Piedmont hazelnuts which have a great flavor.

Matsuhisa Cabernet Sauce

serves 20
21½ fluid ounces (600ml) Matsuhisa Cabernet
3¾ ounces (110g) granulated sugar
1 cinnamon stick
1 vanilla bean (pod), split and the seeds scraped out

Put all the ingredients in a pan and simmer over a medium heat. You will know when it is ready as, after simmering for some time, the sauce will become syrupy. Strain.

Chocolate Sticks

Melt some sweetened chocolate. Pour the chocolate in a thin layer on to a marble board and allow to cool. Use the edge of a large palette knife to scrape the chocolate into long rolls.

TO SERVE

Chocolate chips
berries (such as raspberries, blueberries, etc.)
chervil sprigs

1 Finish the Layered Hazelnut Cake by spooning the caramel ice cream on to the hazelnut wafers. Spread the ice cream out with a palette knife. Do this 3 times to make triple layered wafers and finish with a final wafer. Chill well again so that the layered cake is easy to slice cleanly.
2 Pour the Matushisa Cabernet Sauce on to plates. Scatter the Hazelnut Succès, roast hazelnuts, chocolate chips, and the berries on the sauce.
3 Cut the Layered Hazelnut Cake into 2-inch (6cm) slices, and arrange three on each plate leaning against one another. Decorate with chocolate sticks and chervil.

ユズスープ　冬瓜と季節のフルーツ　杏仁アイスクリーム添え
Yuzu Soup with Apricot Ice Cream

A winter melon compote is given the "yuzu soup treatment" and lavished with seasonal fruits.

Yuzu Soup

serves 4

6¾ fluid ounces (200ml) freshly squeezed yuzu
   juice and grated peel of ⅕ yuzu
6¾ fluid ounces (200ml) mineral water
5¼ ounces (150g) granulated sugar
¾ ounce (25g) kuzu
2 tablespoons and 2 teaspoons Matsuhisa
   Chardonnay
2 tablespoons Hokusetsu saké

1　Put the yuzu juice in a pan with the mineral water and sugar. Bring to a boil. Thicken with the kuzu dissolved in a little water. Stir over medium heat for 1 minute.
2　Strain the thickened yuzu soup into a bowl, cover with plastic wrap, and chill in the fridge.
3　When the soup has chilled, add the Chardonnay, Hokusetsu sake, and the grated yuzu peel.

Apricot Ice Cream

serves 4

10½ fluid ounces (300ml) milk
10½ fluid ounces (300ml) fresh whipping cream
4 ounces (110g) granulated sugar
½ ounce (15g) apricot powder or essence
1 tablespoon Amaretto liqueur
1 teaspoon apricot flavoring

1　Combine the milk, fresh cream, and sugar in a pan and heat. Turn the heat off just before the mixture comes to a boil. Stir in the apricot powder and dissolve. Then strain and chill.
2　When chilled, add the Amaretto liqueur and apricot flavoring. Put in an ice-cream maker and freeze.

Winter Melon Compote

serves 4

¼ large firm winter melon
3½ ounces (100g) granulated sugar
   LYCHEE SYRUP
   18 fluid ounces (500ml) water
   10 ounces (275g) granulated sugar
   2 tablespoons lychee liqueur

1　Make the lychee syrup: bring all the ingredients to a boil in a pan and then allow to cool.
2　Cut out the melon flesh with a large melon baller.
3　Heat 1 quart (1 litre) water and the sugar in a pan. After it comes to a boil, reduce the heat to low. Add the melon, cover with plastic wrap and continue to simmer over a low heat until the melon turns semi-translucent. When the melon reaches this state, rinse once with cold water.
4　Soak the cooked winter melon in the cool lychee syrup for at least half a day before use.

NOBU'S NOTE
*　As this needs to soak for at least half a day it is probably best to make it the day before.

TO SERVE

seasonal fruits
sprig of mint

Put the Apricot Ice Cream in a deep dish. Spread with the Winter Melon Compote and seasonal fruits. Pour over the Yuzu Soup. Garnish with a sprig of mint.

NOBU'S NOTE
*　Fruits that go well with this might include watermelon, melon, mango, lychees, or others of the melon family or similar fruits. Remember you are making a "soup" dish here. Hard fruits will not go well with it.

フルーツ酒
Fruit Saké

These three vividly colored, deeply translucent fruit sakés are especially popular with the ladies.

Mango Saké

serves 12

1.8 quarts (1.8 litres) Hokusetsu saké (pure rice)

7 ounces (200g) sugar syrup

10½ ounces (300g) mango flesh

3 tablespoons and 1 teaspoon mango syrup

10 drops ginger juice, squeezed from the root in a
    garlic press

1   Add a little Japanese saké to the syrup and
fresh mango, put into a juicer and blend.

2   Add the mango syrup and ginger juice, then
strain through a cloth. Add the remaining saké and
store in the fridge.

Melon Saké

serves 12

21½ ounces (600g) completely ripe musk melon
    flesh

10 mint leaves, chopped

1.8 quarts (1.8 litres) Hokusetsu saké (pure rice)

2 tablespoons and 2 teaspoons lemon juice

sugar syrup

10½ fluid ounces (300ml) Midori melon liqueur

1   Put the melon and chopped mint leaves into a
mixer, add a little Japanese saké, and mix to a juice.
If insufficiently sweet, add some syrup.

2   Sieve thoroughly through a fine cloth, then add
the lemon juice and the melon liqueur. Store in the
fridge.

Strawberry Saké

serves 12

1.8 quarts (1.8 litres) Hokusetsu saké (pure rice)

25 strawberries, stems removed

peel of 1 lemon

3½ ounces (100g) sugar lumps

2 cinnamon sticks

5 cloves

1   Put all the ingredients in a covered pot and allow
to stand at room temperature for a week.

2   Strain before serving.

NOBU'S NOTES

•   Make sure the lid is firmly in place so that none
    of the alcohol escapes.

•   Serve the sakés in a clear bottle or jug so that
    the colors can be appreciated.

s a u

d r e s

s a

NOBU MATSUHISA TALKS ABOUT HIS APPROACH TO WORK

My philosophy has always been that there is little value in a restaurant where joy does not exist at every level. What are customers looking for when they come to a restaurant? They are places we go to eat, so the taste of the food is naturally important, as are the atmosphere and service. But customers come for more than that. They come for the lively demeanor and smiling faces of the staff, the attention to detail, the design of the restaurant, the furniture and fittings. These are the essential elements, the building blocks from which an establishment grows. A vibrant energy pervades every corner of a successful restaurant. They say that customers make a judgement about a restaurant the moment they walk through the door.

Those serving must enjoy what they do. This is crucial. If they are not happy, how can the staff expect their customers to enjoy the experience? It is not enough for a chef to think solely about cooking if he wants happy customers. There is the all-important question of how to ensure the customers really enjoy themselves.

For me it means standing in an open kitchen, watching the faces of the diners, thinking about what to prepare next to keep them happy. The ability to see what's going on and make instant decisions. It's all about enthusiasm. I have been conscious of this in my work from the beginning.

A chef should not become emotionally or mentally stressed. It can only deplete his energy. My rule is that if a chef is under stress, he cannot prepare or serve excellent food.

The success of a restaurant depends on the overall balance of every element of the business, including the management. If all an owner-chef thinks about is the bottom line, and he doesn't really enjoy managing, then important jobs which need his attention will inevitably be neglected. He may go to the trouble of buying in fine ingredients, but will then fail to make good use of the materials. Unless you make good use of the ingredients, there is no way you can produce delicious food. The faces of chefs like this tell the story. They are inevitably stiff and inflexible. Poorly managed restaurants like this are hardly places where customers will enjoy themselves. They will simply take their custom elsewhere.

A relaxed chef, on the other hand, is potentially two or three times more effective in his job. A chef taking pleasure in what he does will naturally affect the atmosphere in the restaurant, and his happiness will be communicated to the customers. Customers will want to come back to the restaurant. The number of repeat clients will increase, and they will bring their friends and acquaintances. Word will get around. The restaurant will prosper. The whole atmosphere will become increasingly lively. One thing leads to another as the business takes off. The restaurant will brim with excitement. This is the sort of "enthusiasm" I am talking about.

The best sort of background music a restaurant can have is that excitement, that buzz. We do not play music in our restaurants. There is simply no need. We do fine with discussion and taste, with customers enjoying the food and the chat. Everyone goes about things differently of course, but we feel there is no need to play background music in our restaurants. The cooks, the staff, and the customers together make a harmonious ensemble. Together we make music. Restaurants are not so much places where those who serve stand on one side and those who are served on the other. All the players together create a symphony. This is the picture I keep in mind.

In essence, I focus on creating the sort of restaurants in which customers can truly enjoy themselves. For the two or three hours that customers come to one of our establishments, we play them the finest 'music'. This is what our restaurants are all about. It is a philosophy which Nobu restaurants around the world embrace.

Glossary

AJI AMARILLO
This dried chili is orange, wrinkled, and tapers to a point. Its fruity flavor makes it suitable for chili sauces and stews. Aji amarillo paste is available as a commercial product in stores selling ingredients for South American cooking.

AJI PANCA
This dried chili is dark brown, wrinkled, and tapers to a point. Its berry flavor and fruit tones make it suitable for chili sauces and fish dishes. Aji panca paste is available as a commercial product in stores selling ingredients for South American cooking.

ANTI-CUCHO
A Peruvian dish. Beef heart is marinated in a red sauce, skewered and grilled over charcoal while being basted with oil. The meat is served with a yellow sauce and eaten with a salsa. (See page 242)

AONORI LAVER
Green seaweed, see Nori.

ASARI CLAMS
Also known as the Manila or short-necked clam, these small clams are very popular in Japan for their tenderness and sweetness.

ASATSUKI CHIVES
Similar to Chinese chives and scallions (spring onions), asatsuki chives (*Allium ledebourianum*) can be shallow-fried as a vegetable or used as seasoning with sashimi.

AYU
This river fish (*Plecoglossus altivelis*) is caught with rod and line from June through August. Large specimens can be as long as 12 inches (30cm), but most are not even half that size. Ayu is usually eaten grilled or broiled with salt.

AYU TADE
A peppery herb often used in the cooking of the ayu river fish. See Tade.

BAMBOO SHOOT SKIN
Known as *take-no-ko* in Japanese, the shoots of both the *Phyllostachys heterocycla* and *P. bambusoides* are a popular delicacy in Japan. The skin, which is usually peeled away before the shoots are boiled, can be used as an attractive garnish with strong hints of late spring, as are the plant's leaves.

BAYBERRIES
The purplish red fruit of the bayberry tree (*Myrica rubra*) is in season from late June to early July. The berries can be eaten raw, pickled in salt or made into jam or a liqueur.

BLACK COD
Also known as sablefish, black cod (*Anoplopoma fimbria*) is a dark-colored marine fish which is caught in North American Pacific waters from the Bering Sea to Isla Cedros, Baja California. Black cod can reach a length of 3 feet (90cm) and average 20 pounds (9kg) in weight. Due to its rich oil content, it is exceptionally flavorful and an excellent fish for smoking. Despite its name, this fish is not in fact actually a member of the cod family.

BLACK RICE
Black rice is a glutinous and ancient variety of Japanese rice with a purple-black pigment in the rice bran. It has a concentrated flavor.

BONITO FLAKES
Filleted bonito is steamed, dried, smoked and cured with a mold (*Aspergillus glaucus*). When the fillets have become as hard as a piece of wood, they are shaved. This whole process takes many months. The flakes are used to make dashi and as a flavoring and garnish in numerous other dishes. In fact, dried bonito flakes are necessary in one way or another for making every Japanese meal. Called *katsuobushi* in Japanese.

BUCKWHEAT
Called soba in Japanese, this herbaceous plant (*Fagopyrum esculentum*) is cultivated for its groats. The husk is removed and used as a filling for pillows. The groats are ground into the flour that is used to make soba noodles. Groats can also be cooked with rice or used for making beer or vodka.

CHILI GARLIC SAUCE
This fiery sauce is made from a blend of fresh, roasted or dried chilies and garlic, sugar, salt, vinegar and other seasonings. Called *tobanjan* in Japanese.

DAIKON
The giant white radish (*Raphanus sativus*) is an essential ingredient in the Japanese larder. Grated daikon is added to the tempura dipping sauce because it aids the digestion of oily foods. Daikons are often cut lengthways into a continuous sheet, using a special grater called a *katsuramuki*, for use in various preparations.

DASHI
Japanese stock is made from dried bonito flakes and konbu. With soy sauce, saké and miso, it is one of the most important elements in Japanese cooking. (See page 97.)

EDAMAME
This is the Japanese term for fresh green soy beans.

ENOKI MUSHROOMS
This winter mushroom (*Flammulina velutipes*) grows naturally worldwide, yet is known almost exclusively by its Japanese name. The sticky yellow-white cap is seldom wider than half an inch (1cm), while the long, thin stalks are usually well over 5 inches (12cm). Enoki mushrooms are used in soups, stews, and grilled with chicken. Fresh enoki are exported from Japan in sealed plastic packets that keep them fresh for a time.

ERINGI MUSHROOMS (*PLEUROTE DU PANICAUT*)
Pleurotus eryngii is a wild mushroom with a dark brown cap to be found between June and October, growing to a height of between 3 and 8 inches (7–20cm). Its flesh is firm and fragrant.

FILO
Filo is the Greek name for a paper-thin pastry used in many desserts from baklava to strudel. It is available already shredded and frozen from commercial suppliers.

FLYING FISH ROE
Also known as tobiko caviar, the tiny, bright orange, salted eggs of the flying fish have a mild, sweet, fishy flavor. Flying fish roe is used in small amounts as a tasty and decorative garnish for sushi and salads.

FRUIT TOMATOES
Also known as sugar or perfect tomatoes, these small, sweet tomatoes can only be produced under special cultivation conditions which restrict the amount of water they are given. The yield is minimal, but their sugar content is as high as any fruit. Fruit tomatoes are not currently exported to the United States and Europe, and have been available in Japan for about ten years.

GARI
Thinly sliced ginger marinated in sweetened rice vinegar is served as a condiment in sushi restaurants so diners can refresh their taste buds between different types of sushi.

GINAAN NUTS
Better known by their Chinese name gingko, these buff-coloured delicate, sweet nuts are popular in Japanese cooking.

GOURD SHAVINGS
Known as *kanpyo*, strips or ribbons cut from the flesh of bottle gourds are sold dried. When rehydrated in lukewarm water they are a popular sushi filling.

HAJIKAMI
These pickled ginger shoots are used to garnish many Japanese meals.

HAMO
The complex meaty flavour of conger eel makes it a prized ingredient in Japanese cuisine. Filleting it is one of the great arts of the Japanese kitchen.

ICE FISH
The odd-looking ghostly Antarctic ice fish is related to the much sought after Chilean sea bass or Patagonian toothfish and has some of its fine distinctive flavour.

ISE LOBSTER
This famed spiny lobster with a long beard and bent back is held to bring long life and wisdom. Festivals are held in honor of the delicacy.

ISHIGAKI (GIANT) CLAMS
The waters around the Japanese island of Ishigaki are famed for their giant clams.

ITO-TOGARASHI
Togarashi is the Japanese for "peppers", and ito means "thread", thus ito-togarashi are long chilies cut lengthways into long fine threads for use as a garnish.

JUNSAI
Sometimes called "water shield" in English, this tiny aquatic plant (*Brasenia schreberi*) has long, thread-like stems that grow up from the root. In early summer, the Japanese harvest the water shield's leafy shoots on the surface of ponds and pools. Junsai is sold loose in plastic bags or in bottles.

KAIWARE DAIKON
The young shoots of the daikon are used in salads and as a garnish for sushi. Cut off the root ends before using these sharp, spicy shoots.

KATAKURIKO

The leaves and flowers of the dogtooth violet (*Erythronium japonicum*) are commonly used as a garnish in Japanese cooking. Flour made from the plant is much prized as a starch and is sometimes used as an expensive alternative to potato flour.

KINKI

Known in English as the bighand thornyhead, this large red fish is a species of alfonsino (*Beryx decadactylus*) or bream.

KINOKO MUSHROOMS

Literally meaning "child of a tree", kinoko is the word for 'mushroom' in Japanese, but the term tends to be used mostly as a generic for wild mushrooms.

KINOME

Sansho sprigs are called *kinome* in Japanese. These young leaves are used as an edible garnish, chopped herb, or made into a paste. (See Sansho.)

KOBE BEEF

Kobe beef is a special grade of beef from cattle raised in Kobe, Japan. The cattle are massaged with sake and fed a daily diet that includes large amounts of beer. This produces meat that is extraordinarily tender, finely marbled, and full-flavored. It is also extremely expensive. Because of the high cost and increasing demand, there are now some Kobe-style beef-cattle being raised in the USA, Australia and Scotland using the same techniques; this is often called waygu beef after the breed of cattle used.

KOCHUJANG

This is a thick, miso-like fermented chili bean paste popular in Korean cuisine. Made from soybean paste, red pepper powder, and glutinous rice flour, it keeps almost indefinitely in the refrigerator. Some brands are hotter than others.

KONBU

Konbu (*Laminaria japonica*) is a variety of kelp that grows in the cold seas off the coast of northern Japan, mostly around the northern part of Hokkaido. Rich in monosodium glutamate, konbu is sold in supermarkets as dashi konbu in fairly large pieces for use in making stock. This konbu should never be washed because the flavor lies on the surface. At most, wipe it clean with a cloth and don't leave it in boiling water. Konbu is also a well-known dietary source of iodine and rich in iron.

KOYARI SQUID

See Aori Squid.

KUZU

Also seen as *kudzu*, this is an Oriental vegetable, the roots of which are generally dried and ground into a powder that is used both as a thickener and as a coating for food being deep-fried.

LOTUS ROOT

The underwater roots of the lotus water lily may be up to 4 foot long and are generally about 2 inches (5cm) in diameter. Peeling their reddish-brown skin reveals creamy-white flesh with a crisp texture and a coconut-like flavor. The roots are available fresh, canned, dried, and candied.

MADAKO OCTOPUS

The common octopus (Octopus vulgarus) reaches an average size of 24–36 inches (60–90cm) in length. Called madako in Japanese, it can be found throughout the world's warm seas.

MAITAKE MUSHROOMS

This autumn mushroom (*Grifola fondosa*) is fragrant, tasty and very versatile. It is best in a preparation called *maitake no kurumi* in which the mushrooms are dressed with a walnut paste.

MAKOMO-DAKE

Known in the West as water bamboo or Manchurian wild rice; this plant belongs to the same family as the common bamboo and is closely related to the wild rice of North America. The enlarged stems are harvested, the upper leaves cut off, and only the stem with husk-like wrapper leaves sent to market. The edible portion is the succulent stem after the husks are removed.

MANTIS SHRIMP

Actually unrelated to shrimp, these crustaceans are referred to as shrimp because of their front appendages and how they use them to capture food. The description "mantis" is due to the fact they resemble the appearance and have the same hunting characteristics of a praying mantis insect. Mantis shrimp are popular in Japanese cuisine and often eaten as sushi.

MATSUTAKE MUSHROOMS

Of the many kinds of edible mushrooms that grow in Japan, matsutake mushrooms are said to be the king, because of their wonderful aroma and flavor. Matsutake grow in the red pine forests in the autumn, and are a special and very expensive delicacy in Japan at that time.

MIRIN

This liquid flavoring containing 14% alcohol is used in cooking for its sweetness rather than its alcoholic content. Regular saké cannot be substituted for it.

MIRU (GIANT) CLAMS

The Japanese term for the white surf clam. It has a mild, sweet flavor.

MISO

This fermented paste of soybeans and either rice or barley with salt is an essential ingredient in the Japanese larder. It is combined with dashi in miso soup and also used as a flavoring for other foods. Red miso, Japan's most popular rice miso, is salty and rich in protein; white miso, on the other hand, is rather sweet. Made from fermented soybeans and barley, moromi miso is never used for making miso soup. This soft, dark brown paste is usually eaten with chilled cucumber.

MIZUNA

This feathery, delicate salad green (*Brassica campeatris*) is a mildly peppery potherb that has been cultivated in Japan since antiquity.

MOLOKHEIYA

This is Egyptian Spinach or melokhai and has a bright green leaf with a soft texture when eaten. In both Mid-Eastern and Asian cultures it is widely used in soups.

MOMIJI-OROSHI

This is a preparation consisting of grated daikon mixed with red-hot chili pepper. It can be bought ready-made or you can make it yourself quite easily by inserting seeds from a chili into a daikon on the tip of a chopstick and then grating the whole thing.

MONGO CUTTLEFISH

The common cuttlefish (*Sepia officinalis*) and the pharaoh cuttlefish (*S. pharaonis*) are both called *mongo ika* in Japanese. The former grows to a maximum length of about 10 inches (25cm) and is familiar in the Mediterranean and east Atlantic. The latter is slightly larger and is prevalent from the Arabian Peninsula across to Japan and Australia.

MOROMI MISO

A type of miso made from fermented barley, but never used for making miso soup. This soft, dark brown paste is most often eaten with chilled cucumber.

MYOGA GINGER

Because only the stems and buds of myoga ginger (*Zingiber mioga*) are eaten, it is hardly recognizable as a type of ginger. It isn't hot like regular ginger and its fragrance is more herbal. The buds are especially aromatic when thinly sliced and used as a garnish.

NIGARI

Nigari, or bittern, is a concentrated solution of various salts remaining after the crystallization of salt from seawater. The main ingredient should generally be magnesium chloride. Nigari is used as the natural solidifying agent in the preparation of tofu.

NIKIRI-ZAKE

This sauce for sushi may be bought or made by mixing one part sake to 3-4 parts shoyu.

NORI

Red laver – asakusa nori – is harvested and dried in paper-thin sheets of a standard size. The nori is then toasted and used for wrapping sushi rolls, rice balls and futomaki. Green laver – aonori – is harvested, dried and sold in tiny flakes to sprinkle over food. Aonori is also an ingredient of shichimi togarashi.

PÂTE BRIQUE

This thin pastry originally comes from North Africa. The dough – consisting of water, flour, salt and vegetable oil – is boiled, making the surface rough, like a brick. Also called *feuilles de briques*, they are sold in circular sheets.

PEN SHELL CLAMS

Also known as fan shell clam or mussel, this is a type of razor clam found embedded in the mud. Once highly popular in Japan, they are now becoming rather rare and highly prized.

PONZU

A citrus-and-soy-sauce dip (see page 63).

RED MISO

Red miso (*akamiso*) is made from a fermented paste of soybeans and rice. It is red to brown in color and high in protein and salt.

RED VINEGAR

This sweet and powerful rice vinegar made with saké lees that have been fermented with yeast and the koji mold for three years is the preferred choice of sushi chefs, because relatively little sugar is needed to make the shari-zu for vinegared sushi rice.

RICE VINEGAR

All vinegar produced in Japan is fermented from rice and is mild in flavor, with about 4.2% acidity. Non-rice vinegars cannot be used as substitutes.

ROCK SHRIMP

So-called because of their rock-hard shells, rock shrimp are valued for their lobster-like texture and flavor.

ROCOTO CHILI PASTE

Also known as rocotillo, this relation of the habañero is orange-yellow or deep red when ripe, round with furrows, and tapering to a point. It is mildly fruity and has an intense heat. Essential for ceviches, rocoto chili paste is available as a commercial product in stores selling ingredients for South American cooking.

SANSHO

The seedpods of the Japanese pepper (*Zanthoxylum piperitum*) are ground and used as seasoning, especially as one of the seven spices in shichimi togarashi. The sansho is usually sold ground, as it keeps its fragrance quite well. Sansho sprigs (the young leaves are called *kinome* in Japanese) can be used as an edible garnish, chopped herb, or made into a paste.

SHAKKIRI MUSHROOMS

This wild mushroom (*Agrocybe cylindracea*) is found at the foot of willow and maple trees between spring and fall. It has a dark brown cap and grows to a height of between 4 and 6 inches (10–15cm). Its flesh is firm and crisp. Marketed as the shakkiri mushroom, nowadays it is cultivated and sold throughout the year.

SHICHIMI TOGARASHI

This "seven-spice mixture" is a snappy collection of seven dried and ground flavors: red pepper flakes, roughly ground sansho, tiny flakes of mandarin orange peel, black hemp seeds, tiny flakes of green nori and white sesame seeds. Available in three strengths – mild, medium and hot – from Asian supermarkets.

SHIITAKE MUSHROOMS

The best-known Japanese mushroom (*Lentinus edodes*) is extensively cultivated and often available in its dried form. Its distinctive pungent flavor goes well with Japanese food. Fresh shiitake are good as tempura, in stews or simply grilled with a little salt.

SHIMEJI MUSHROOMS

This autumn mushroom (*Lycophyllum shimeji*) is known for its excellent flavor rather than its aroma. It has straw-colored caps about 1/4 inch (1cm) in diameter. Shimeji come in clumps that grow from a single stem, like miniature oyster mushrooms, at the base of pine trees. Cooking them releases a distinctive flavor and aroma, making them very suitable for soups and other simmered dishes, as well as mixed rice dishes.

SHISO

There are both red and green shiso leaves. The red ones (*akajiso*) are mainly used to color umeboshi and other pickles. The green leaves (*aojiso*) have many uses as a herb, tempura and garnish. Although it is called a perilla or beefsteak plant (*Perilla frutescens*) in English, shiso is actually a member of the mint family. Shiso buds are also used as a condiment, garnish and, when very young, for tempura.

SNOW CRAB

This large crab (*Chionoecetes opilio*) is caught in the Sea of Japan in the winter months and served as sashimi, tempura and in vinegared preparations. Snow crab meat is sweet and delicate, with a more fibrous texture than king crab. Its texture ranges from the tender longitudinal fibers of shoulder meat to the firmer fibers of claw meat.

SOBA

Buckwheat noodles can be eaten either hot or cold. In their simplest form, a dashi-based soup is poured over the boiled noodles for kake-soba. When eaten cold, the noodles are served on a bamboo sieve with a dipping sauce. This is called *zaru-soba* (zaru being the Japanese for bamboo sieve).

SOMEN

These dried, fine wheat noodles are served cold with a chilled dipping sauce usually in the summer. The noodles are boiled very briefly and then immediately refreshed in cold water.

SU-MISO

White miso paste thinned with rice vinegar is often used as a dressing.

SUDACHI

This acidic citrus fruit (*Citrus sudachi*) is a smaller relative of yuzu. It is used in the summer and autumn while still green for its tangy juice and aromatic zest. Sudachi is rarely available outside Japan and lemons can be used as a substitute.

TADE

This is the water pepper, smartweed or knotweed plant (*Polygonum hydropiper*). The tiny leaves have a mild peppery flavor and are much used as a garnish for sashimi. The leaves and stems may also be cooked and eaten, and these and the seeds are often made into peppery condiments.

TATAMI-IWASI (DRY-FOLDED SARDINES)

Sold as sheets and looking a little like thin dried noodles, these are tiny baby sardines that have been quickly pressed and dried. They are used both as a crisp tasty snack and as a flavoring.

TIRADITO

Tiradito is a South American dish consisting of cut fish and ceviche seasonings. Its name is derived from *tirar* (the Spanish for "throw") because the fish slices are thrown into the serving bowl.

TOMYO PEA SPROUTS

Chinese pea shoots (*dau miui* and *dou miao*) are the handpicked, tender leaves and stems of the snow or garden pea plants, and are used as a light seasoning or added to soups. In Japan, tomyo pea sprouts are cultivated hydroponically and produced throughout the year in bulk. Pea sprouts are more aromatic and delicately flavored than bean sprouts.

TORO

The belly of tuna is very pale in color and fatty. Highly prized for sushi and sashimi, it is considered the best cut of the fish.

UDO

The white stalks and leaves of this aromatic plant (*Aralia cordata*) are similar to asparagus in taste. The tender young stems can be eaten raw or boiled.

UDON

These soft, thick wheat noodles are eaten in a dashi-based soup with tempura and other accompaniments.

WAKAME

This seaweed (*Undaria pinnitifida*) is used in miso soup, salads and other dishes.

WASABI

Although similar in flavor, Japanese horseradish (*Wasabia japonica*) is less harsh and more fragrant than its English cousin. Fresh wasabi is very expensive. It grows wild in cool, shallow pools of pure water, often high in the mountains, and is extensively cultivated under similar conditions. It can also be bought as a powder or paste from Asian supermarkets.

WHITE MISO

White miso (*shiromiso*) is made from a fermented paste of soybeans and rice or barley. It is beige to light brown in color and quite sweet. A high-grade Kyoto product, white miso is expensive.

YAMAGOBO ROOT

The young, edible roots of a woodland thistle called mori azami (*Cirsium dipsacolepis*) bear a striking resemblance to burdock, even though there is no direct relation between these flora. Yamagobo roots are typically pickled in miso or soy sauce and used as a filling in futomaki and other sushi rolls.

YAMA-MOMO

The Japanese term for the bayberry (*Myrica rubra*).

YARIIKA SQUID

Yariika or spear squid (*Loligo bleekeri*) is a slender, spear-shaped cephalopod which grows to about 15 inches (40cm) in length. Spear squid are caught in the seas around Japan, particularly in the spring when they come close to the coast to lay their eggs.

YUBA

The skin that forms on the surface of soy milk when heated is the richest known source of protein (over 50%) and similarly high in natural sugars and polyunsaturated fats. Eaten both fresh and dried, most yuba is made in Kyoto and can be quite expensive.

YUZU

Japanese citron (*Citrus junos*) is zestier than lemons and not as sweet. Yuzu also has a very potent fragrance. It is used for both its acidic juice and its aromatic rind. Yuzu juice is now available from Asian supermarkets.

YUZU KOSHO

Available from Japanese markets, this commercial seasoning comprises green chili, yuzu rind and salt.

Index

A

Abalone:
   Somen and Junsai Cold Soup 90, 91
   Tempura 114-15, 116
Aji amarillo 250
Aji panca 250
Ama-zu 36
Ama-zu Ponzu Sauce 103, 104
Anchovies, Home-cured, Bonito Tataki with 81,
   83
Anti-cucho 250
Anti-cucho Sauce:
   Orange 242
   Red 242
Aonori laver 250
Aroz con Pollo 217, 218
Asparagus: Shrimp and, with Egg Sauce 53, 54
Asparagus, White:
   Salad with Watercress Dressing, Watercress
      and 70, 71
   and Sea Bass Sashimi with Mint Dressing 17, 18
Avocado Egg Pudding 128, 129
Ayu 250
   Baby, Soup 96, 97
   Bamboo Roasted, with Green and Red Tade
      Sauce 174, 176
Ayu tade 250

B

Bamboo Jello 222-3, 224-5
Bamboo Roasted Ayu with Green and Red Tade
   Sauces   174, 176
Banana Egg Roll 226, 227-9
Bayberries 250
Beef, Kobe 251
   with Anti-cucho Sauce 166, 167
   New-Style Sashimi 80, 82
   Steak with Baked Eringi Mushrooms 164, 165
Black Pepper Crusted Black Cod 177, 179
Bonito:
   flakes 250
   Tataki with Home-cured Anchovies 81, 83
Broiled Toro Back 180, 182
Brussels Sprouts, Scallop and, with Jalapeño
   Salsa 157, 159
Buckwheat 250

C

Cabbage, Chinese, Steak 148, 149
Cake, Hazelnut Layered 233, 234û5
'Californian chawan-mushi' 128, 129
Caramel Ice Cream 234
Carpaccio, Nobu's Octopus 29, 30
Caviar:
   Monkfish Pâté with, and Vinegar Mustard
      Sauce 19, 19
   Pen Shell Clam with 28, 30
   Sweet Shrimp Tartar with 25, 27
Ceviche:
   Fruit Tomato and Vegetable 34, 36
   Hot 50-1, 52
   Sauce 243
Cherry Jello 223, 225
Chicken Grilled, with Wasabi Pepper Sauce 181,
   183
Chips:
   Baby Spinach, Grilled Salmon with 175, 176

Fish Skin 119, 121
   Lotus Root, with Tuna and White Fish 20-1, 24
Chives, asatsuki 250
Chocolate:
   Ice Cream 228
   Macaroons 228
   Sauce 229
   Sticks 235
Cilantro Sauce 60-1, 62
Clams:
   Asari 250
   Ishigaki 250
   Miru 251
   and Yuba Sauté 160, 161
   Pen Shell 251
   with Caviar 28, 30
   Razor, Sautéed 145, 147
Coconut Nage 232
Cod, Black 250
   Black Pepper Crusted 177, 179
   with Miso 169, 171
Compote, Winter Melon 237
Crab, King:
   Claw, Tempura with Butter Ponzu Sauce 103,
      104
   with Creamy Spicy Sauce 153, 154
   Tempura with Sweet and Sour Ponzu Sauce
      103, 105
   White Soufflé with Truffle 156, 159
Crab, snow 252
Crab, Soft Shell:
   Deep-fried, with Cactus Salsa 100, 102
   Roll 194, 196
Crab, Soft-shell:
   Spring Roll 101, 102
Curry Salt 116
Custard, Chawan-mushi 127
Cuttlefish, mongo 251

D

Daikon 250
   kaiware 251
Dashi 250
Deep-fried Halibut Cheek with Black Pepper Chili
   Garlic Sauce 150, 152
Deep-fried Soft Shell Crab with Cactus Salsa 100,
   102
Deep-fried Toro Tataki with Spicy Garlic Sauce
   53, 55
Don, Kabayaki Sardine 216, 218
Dressings:
   Jalapeño 246
   Matsuhisa 67, 68, 133, 133, 247
   Mint 17, 18
   Spicy Lemon 151, 152, 246
   Watercress 70, 71, 246
   Yuzu 246

E

Edamame 250

F

Filo 250
   Oyster 112, 113
"Fish & Chips", Sea Eel 118, 120
Fish Skin Chips 119, 121
Foie Gras:
   with Japanese Truffle Sauce, Hamo and 140,
      143

with Miso 138, 139
Fritter, Baby Ice Fish 109, 110-11
Fruit Tomato see Tomato, Fruit
Funa Sushi Nobu-Style 198, 199

G

Galettes, Soba 199
Gari 250
Garlic Sauce:
   Black Pepper Chili 152
   Spicy 53, 243
   Lemon 170, 243
Garlic Sautéed Kuruma Shrimp 144, 146
Ginaan nuts 250
Gin'an 127
Ginger, myoga 251
Gourd shavings 250
Grapefruit Sauté 232
Grilled Chicken with Wasabi Pepper Sauce 181,
   183
Grilled Koyari Squid 177, 178
Grilled Salmon with baby Spinach Chips 175, 176

H

Hajikami 250
Halibut:
   Cheek, Deep-fried, with Black Pepper Chili
      Garlic Sauce 150, 152
   Roll 189
Hamo 250
   and Foie Gras with Japanese Truffle Sauce 140,
      143
Hazelnuts:
   Cake, Layered 233, 234-5
   Roasted 235
   Succès 235
   Wafers 234
Horse Mackerel, Sautéed, with Spicy Lemon
   Dressing 151, 152
Hot Ceviche 50, 51

I

Ice Cream:
   Apricot 237
   Caramel 234
   Chocolate 228
   Rock Salt 231
Ice Fish 250
   Baby, Fritter 109, 110-11
Ito-togarashi 250

J

Jalapeño:
   Salsa 157, 159, 247
   Soba 204, 205-7
   and Su-miso Sauce, Toro with 86, 87
Japanese Shad Namban Style 107, 109
Jello:
   Bamboo 222-3, 224-5
   Cherry 223, 225
   Passion Fruit Pasta 231
Junsai 250
   Cold Soup, Abalone Somen and 90, 91

K

Katakuriko 251
Kettle Soup, Matsutake 92, 94
Khakiage, Sea Urchin and Corn 116, 117

Kinki 251
    Yuba Roll, Steamed 134, 135
Kinome 251
Kochujang 251
Konbu 251
Kuzu 251

L
Lamb Chop with Miso Anti-cucho Sauce 172, 173
Lemon Dressing, Spicy 151, 152, 246
Lemon Garlic Sauce, Spicy 170, 243
Lobster, Ise 250
    with Spicy Lemon Garlic Sauce 168, 170
Lobster Inaniwa Pasta Salad 210, 211
Lotus Root 251
    Chips with Tuna and White Fish 20-1, 24

M
Macaroons, Chocolate 228
Mackerel
    Moromi-Miso 131, 132
    see also Horse Mackerel
Makomo-Dake 251
    with Creamy Spicy Sauce 183, 184-5
Mango:
    Pudding 222, 224
    Saké 238, 239
    Sherbet 228
Marinade, Namban 109
Matsuhisa Dressing 247
Matsuhisa Salsa 247
Matsutake Kettle Soup 92, 94
Maui Onion Salsa 247
Melon:
    Saké 238, 239
    Winter, Compote 237
Minced Baby White Shrimp Skewers 48, 49
Mirin 251
Miso 251
    Anti-cucho Sauce 172, 173
    Black Cod with 169, 171
    Dried, Snapper Sashimi with 76, 77
    drying 77, 77
    Foie Gras with 138, 139
    moromi 251
    Mustard 245
    Vinegar Sauce 245
    red 251
    Saikyo Sweet, Nobu-Style 245
    white 252
    see also Su-Miso
Mizuna 251
Molokheiya 251
    Salad, Octopus and 66, 68
Momiji-oroshi 251
Monkfish Pâté with Caviar and Vinegar Mustard
    Sauce 19, 19
Moromi-Miso Mackerel 131, 132
Mushrooms:
    enoki 250
    Eringi 250
    Baked, Kobe Beef Steak with 164, 165
    kinoko 251
    maitake 251
    matsutake 251
    Matsutake Kettle Soup 92, 94
    Shimeji 252
    shiitake 252
    Toban Yaki 153, 155

Mussels and Clams with Nobu's Salsas 32, 33
Mustard Miso 245
Mustard Vinegar Miso Sauce 245

N
Nage, Coconut 232
Nigari 251
Nikiri-zake 251
Nobu's Octopus Carpaccio 29, 30
Nori 251

O
Octopus:
    Baby, Quick Simmered 45, 46
    Carpaccio, Nobu's 29, 30
    madako 251
    and Molokheiya Salad 66, 68
Oyster:
    Filo 112, 113
    Salmon Roll 16, 18
    and Sea Urchin Shooter 37, 37
    Tiradito 78-9, 82

P
Palm Hearts, preparing 25, 25
Parmesan Baked Small Scallops 43, 44
Passion Fruit Pasta 230, 231-2
Pasta:
    Passion Fruit 230, 231-2
    Salad, Lobster Inaniwa 210, 211
Pâté, Monkfish, with Caviar and Vinegar Mustard
    Sauce 19, 19
Pâte brique 251
Pickling Mixture, Nobu-style Saikyo Miso 139
Ponzu 251
Pudding:
    Avocado Egg 128, 129
    Mango 222, 224
    Sea Urchin 124, 125
    Shark's Fin and Sea Urchin 126, 127
    Tofu 222, 224

Q
Quick Simmered Baby Octopus 45, 46

R
Ray Fin with Spicy Black Bean Sauce 130, 132
Rice:
    black 250
    Risotto, Black and Red 214, 215
    vinegar 251
Risotto, Black and Red Rice 214, 215
Rock Salt Ice Cream 231
Rocoto chili paste 251
Roe, flying fish 250
Rolls 188
    Banana Egg 226, 227-9
    Halibut 189
    Kuruma Shrimp 56, 57
    New-Style Salmon 189
    Oyster Salmon 16, 18
    Salmon Kelp 35, 36
    Salmon Skin 195, 196
    Sea Bream 189
    Seared Toro 189
    Shrimp Tempura 189
    Soft Shell Crab 194, 196
    Spicy Tuna 189

Spring, Soft-shell Crab 101
Steamed Kinki Yuba 134, 135
Tuna Sashimi Tempura, with Yuzu Miso Sauce
    40, 41
Vegetable 189
Young Yellowtail 189

S
Saikyo Miso Pickling Mixture, Nobu-style 139
Saké, Fruit 238, 239
Salad:
    Baby Spinach, with Sea Bass 63, 65
    Lobster Inaniwa Pasta 210, 211
    Octopus and Molokheiya 66, 68
    Salmon Skin 72, 73
    Spicy Tuna 63, 64
    Tuna Tataki Sashimi, with Matsuhisa Dressing
        67, 68
    Watercress and White Asparagus, with
        Watercress Dressing 70, 71
Salmon:
    Grilled, with Baby Spinach Chips 175, 176
    Kelp Roll 35, 36
    Roll, New-Style 189
Salmon Skin:
    Roll 195, 196
    Salad 72, 73
Salsas:
    Cactus Leaf 100, 102
    Jalapeño 157, 159, 247
    Matsuhisa 247
    Maui Onion 247
    Nobu's 32, 33
    Vegetable 45, 47
Sansho 252
Sardine, Kabayaki, Don 216, 218
Sashimi:
    Kobe Beef New-Style 80, 82
    Snapper, with Dried Miso 76, 77
    Tempura Roll, Tuna, with Yuzu Miso Sauce 40,
        41
    White Asparagus and Sea Bass, with Mint
        Dressing 17, 18
Sauces:
    Anti-cucho 166, 167
    Black Pepper Chili Garlic 150, 152
    Butter Ponzu 103, 104, 244
    Ceviche 50, 52, 243
    chili garlic 250
    Black Pepper 152
    Chocolate 229
    ·Cilantro 60-1, 62, 208, 209
    Creamy Spicy 106, 108, 153, 154, 183, 184-5,
        242
    Egg 53, 53
    Escargot-style Butter 44
    Green and Red Tade 174, 176
    Jalapeño and Su-miso 86, 87
    Japanese Truffle 140, 143
    Matsuhisa Cabernet 235
    Miso Anti-cucho 172, 173
    Mustard Vinegar Miso 245
    Orange Anti-cucho 242
    Pomodoro 202, 203
    Red Anti-cucho 242
    Shark's Fin Black Bean 141, 143
    Spicy Black Bean 130, 132
    Spicy Garlic 53, 55
    Spicy Lemon Garlic 168, 170